salon management

salon
management

Martin Green

Hairdressing And Beauty Industry Authority

THOMSON

LEARNING™

Australia   Canada   Mexico   Singapore   Spain   United Kingdom   United States

Salon Management

Copyright © Martin Green 2001

The Thomson Learning logo is a registered trademark used herein under licence.

For more information, contact Thomson Learning, Berkshire House, 168–173 High Holborn, London, WC1V 7AA or visit us on the World Wide Web at: http://www.thomsonlearning.co.uk

British Library Cataloguing-in-Publication Data
A catalogue record for this book is available from the British Library

ISBN 1-86152-660-1

First published 2001 Thomson Learning

Printed in Italy by G. Canale & C.

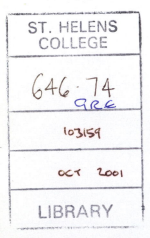

contents

foreword

Exhilarating, frightening, boring, hard work, enjoyable. These are just some of the words that I hear from hair-dressers and beauty therapists. Which word would you choose to describe setting up or running your own business?

Most people start with the best intentions and good ideas but get bogged down with all the paperwork, systems and procedures, rules and regulations. This book from Martin Green, himself an experienced salon owner, puts everything into perspective, giving you facts, tips and a wealth of examples on how to manage your business. What's more the book can be used as a companion to the NVQ/SVQ Level 4 Management qualification.

Running your own salon is rewarding. Invest in this book and see why 'exhilarating' is the first word I used.

Alan Goldsbro
Chief Executive
Hairdressing And Beauty Industry Authority

acknowledgements

The author and publishers would like to thank the following people and organisations for their assistance in producing this book:

Andrew Collinge
Clynol
Computill Ltd
Goldwell
Hairdressers Journal International
Hairdressing And Beauty Industry Authority
L'Oreal
Mahogany
Nationally Approved Salon Campaign
Patrick Cameron
Saks
Sharp
TRESemme
Wella.

The author and publishers also wish to thank the following for permission to use copyright material:

Controller of Her Majesty's Stationery Office for Crown copyright material
Health and Safety Executive
H.M. Customs and Excise
Inland Revenue.

Every effort has been made to trace all the copyright holders but if any have been inadvertently overlooked the publishers will be pleased to make the necessary arrangements at the first opportunity.

introduction

The NVQ level 4 has been long awaited by the industry and over the next few years we can expect a strong take-up by salons in support of this qualification. The managers of today and tomorrow have much to do if the industry is going to be ready to meet the necessary and inevitable changes in the future. Change is not to be feared, it is merely the process of progress and without it our industry will fall back into the dark ages. Managers are the people who cope; they handle situations and scenarios, people and resources.

The industry's survival depends on the development of young employees, on their desire to achieve and to go forward and meet challenges. What is it that encouraged that young creative person to go it alone? Where did they learn employment legislation? How did they cope with accounts? When did they find time to gain management experience and yet still be able to find time to update their own technical skills? If managers have coped without formal training in the past, what will they be able to achieve in the future? Now there are two routes available: our aspiring managers can choose between Management Charter Initiative (MCI standards) or The Small Firms Enterprise Development Initiative (SFEDI standards). Either route, depending upon individual needs, will enable the candidate to gain valuable experience in business commerce and national recognition for their attainments.

This book sets out to provide the fundamental cornerstones of management issues whilst remaining an *aide-mémoire* for existing managers. It will be the good companion for managers of the future.

Martin Green

planning for business

■ the business plan

If you want to start your own business or you are planning the expansion of an existing one you will need money. The most popular source of money is the bank, so how will you persuade the bank to put their faith in you and hand over their money?

A business plan is essentially a unique formula for how a successful business is to be run. The information within the plan should be specific to your business, but should at least address the following areas:

- The purpose and idea
- The market
- Business premises
- Equipment
- Staffing levels
- Set-up costs
- Overheads and cash flow forecast.

writing a business plan

Before you start to write a business plan you need to understand why it is so important. Unfortunately statistics show that one-third of all new business start-ups fail within their first trading year! From the remaining two-thirds, 90 per cent will fail before 5 years have elapsed!

The business plan is the most important document that is produced for any business start-up, therefore a well-thought-out, carefully structured and realistic business plan is your key to success.

You must know your market if you want to achieve your goals and meet the financial targets.

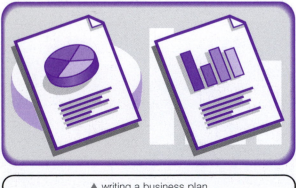

▲ writing a business plan

When do I need to develop a business plan? This will depend on a number of situations:

- *New business venture* – If you are starting a new business you will need to plan and assess the impact that your business will have within the marketplace, as well as demonstrating how you will succeed.
- *Existing business* – If you going to purchase an existing, established business you will need to evaluate the strengths and weaknesses to decide whether this is a viable option for you.
- *Re-financing plan* – If you are already up and running and you need extra finance to develop your business further, you will need to convince others of your plans and continuing success.

The plan, like any book, should be organised in such a way that it follows a logical sequence. It should be written with the reader in mind. The length of the plan will depend on the specific aspects and nature of the business, but even a simple, well-presented plan could extend to 20 pages of A4. For more involved business plans, twice that amount is not uncommon for small businesses.

The professionally drafted plan should follow this type of format:

Table of contents page

Executive summary

Your business idea

Your services, products and/or treatments

Existing market climate

The marketing plan

Your operational plan

Financial forecasts and analysis

Appendices

▲ making a choice

table of contents page

This should be a simple 'at a glance' page illustrating the contents, which allows the reader to navigate the document easily.

the executive summary

This should be a clear and concise statement which will provide your reader with an overview of the business venture. You should incorporate into this summary:

- The current business position (geographical location, trading position etc.)
- Identification of your customers who will be buying your services, and the pattern of repeat sales
- The business objectives, short, medium and long term
- A summary of financial forecasts and expected borrowing.

your business idea

In this section you should explain who you are, what experience you have and what you intend to do. Make sure that you cover the following points:

1. Your name and your business name, along with addresses and telephone numbers
2. The legal status that you will trade under
3. Levels of staffing
4. The business objectives and how they will be achieved
5. Your mission and/or value statement.

the purpose and idea

You will need to explain what you want, why you need it and the use to which the money will be put.

If property purchase or salon refits are involved, remember to include photographs and sketches; your manager will be able to visualise what your plans are. Set realistic objectives – the bank will be interested in your business aims and will be observing your business quite closely, at least for the first year.

sole trader, partnership or limited company?

When you have decided to go into business you will need to choose the legal entity that you will trade under:

- Sole trader
- Partnership
- Limited company.

sole trader

This entity, as the name suggests, is a business where one person who is self-employed is solely responsible for the initiation and subsequent running of the business. The sole trader wholly owns the assets of the firm and receives his remuneration (drawings) from the generated profits. He will pay tax to Inland Revenue, based upon a 'self-assessment', in two instalments each year and is responsible for paying his own national insurance contributions (NICs). This type of business ownership is simple and not complex to set up.

However, the sole trader is personally liable for any debts incurred during the business term and may be pursued personally by his creditors. This can lead to distraint and even bankruptcy (see pages 18–19).

Anyone who operates as a sole trader need only contact their local Inland Revenue office (several leaflets relating to sole traders, self-employment accounting and VAT can be obtained from your local tax enquiry centre).

partnerships

A partnership is similar in some ways to a sole trader inasmuch as it is simple to establish. Each partner has a share in the firm, depending on their proportion of equity. Similarly, the partners (anything between two and twenty individuals) receive drawings made against profits and they handle their tax affairs just like sole traders.

It is strongly advisable to draw up a contract in the event of a partnership. Problems can occur and unless an agreement exists at the beginning, setting out the specific terms of ownership, the responsibility of liability for partners may seem unfair. This can be particularly difficult if one partner incurs debts. In legal terms the partners are jointly and severally liable, which means that one or more partners can be liable

for the recovery of the whole debt although they may not have had anything to do with the one 'rogue' partner's losses!

Sole traders and partnerships are not required to publish their accounts.

limited companies

These are the most complex to set up. When a company is formed it becomes a separate entity from its owner(s). A company (limited or not) is controlled by shares; the individuals that own it are only financially responsible for paying for the shares they are issued with. Limited companies employ the people that work for them. Therefore the directors are paid under PAYE and the company pays the NICs as well as corporation tax upon the profits.

There are distinct advantages and disadvantages in forming a company and anyone considering this should consult their professional advisors.

key personnel

You will need to state the business staff requirement. Remember to incorporate the junior as well as the senior staff. If you have prepared job descriptions you can make reference to them here, although they will need to be kept within the appendices.

If the nature of your business requires specialist technicians, provide details of the range and levels of expertise that you expect to employ.

Within your staffing details, provide details of your intended staff, their work roles and the services that you are going to offer. Give your reader your intentions relating to expected levels of ability and experience. Build into your plan the details of pay formulas, salaries, commissions and incentives schemes.

define your business objectives

Your business objectives should provide a blueprint for you to work with. Once they have been identified you are then able to measure the business effectiveness against them. It is very important to define your objectives from the outset, as this will show that you have considered the long-term future and direction of the business, whilst providing periods when they can be clearly assessed.

Everyone's objectives will be different – some will seem simple, others may be quite complex. Whatever you identify as your objectives, make sure that you can substantiate these statements with facts and figures. Remember objectives should be achievable and measurable.

short-term objectives

Your short-term objectives should relate to your initial twelve months of trading since they provide the foundation of the business activity. If they have been thought about carefully, they should be listed in order of attainment. Realistically, few businesses make a profit in their first year, so you may want to show how borrowing will be reduced, or how the client database should be growing.

medium-term objectives

The medium term should reflect the first couple of years. You need not give a list of objectives in the same detail as you did for your short-term planning, but you will probably indicate the continued growth in sales volumes, or regular customers, whilst maintaining the reduction of borrowing.

long-term objectives

The long-term objectives should identify, say, a three-year plan; this may look to future expansion, more staff and the introduction of new services or treatments. In reality, the long-term objectives reflect the expected direction of the firm and would need to be stated in more general terms.

the mission statement

The mission statement should provide a short and easy-to-understand business philosophy; it exists to show others that your business has a specific purpose. Some companies spend a fortune devising suitable mission statements and sometimes they have to modify them as their strategy changes.

In essence, a mission statement should provide a concise statement telling others what you want to achieve. For example, the British Airways' mission statement is 'To be the world's favourite airline'.

A well-drafted mission statement should state:

■ what business you are in
■ a clear long-term goal
■ how it will be achieved, reflecting standard or quality.

services, products and/or treatments

This section details the range of services, products and treatments you will provide. Give the reader a full description of the services that you intend to offer, the treatments that you will provide, and the range and variety of products that you will use. If you have already negotiated with a manufacturer or wholesaler about your supplies, add some illustrations and costings. When providing technical information, remember to simplify or provide further explanation of what your terms mean; remember your reader is not a salon owner and these aspects are vital to your future success, so spend some time compiling this information.

existing market climate

This section should give a full evaluation of your existing competitors and the market you are in. You need to identify your customers and why they will want your services as opposed to the existing services provided by your competitors. Unless you can show that you have a thorough understanding of the present market climate, your business plan will be a 'non-starter'.

define your market

You know the business that you are in. You can only assess your potential by researching the existing levels of provision. Research your competitors and your customers. Market segmentation is the key: it is unlikely that you will be able to provide all things to all people, but within a total market there are specific groups that you will want to reach. See pages 25–36 for more information.

You should be able to identify the profile of your customers; this will include ages, income groups, their hairdressing needs and their average individual spend. You will need to know your products and operating environment, as well as the monthly and annual expected income and how you plan to tackle your competitors.

the marketing plan

The marketing plan should describe how you will reach, promote and sell your services to your identified targets. This will cover details of:

1. market research
2. who your target market is
3. the competition
4. marketing methods.

You will find a comprehensive text relating to marketing on pages 25–36. In essence, your business plan must contain your marketing plan. You will have already established exactly where and how big your potential market is. The next thing will be turning your findings into a specific range of marketing objectives. The plan will lay the foundations for how you intend to promote your business, ensuring your success in generating sales volumes.

the operational plan

The operational plan should explain how the business will run successfully and profitably. It should provide details of how you selected the correct business premises. There is an old marketing saying which relates to retail shops: 'The three most important things in business are – location, location and location'. The business position in relation to reaching your market is everything. Where you are positioned in relation to your competition will have a direct impact upon your business.

Define your standards of quality. In manufacturing there are specific quality standards that, once attained, act as a precursor in letting potential customers know the calibre of people that they are dealing with. Conversely, the standards that you aspire to should be commensurate with your costings. To put it another way: it would be pointless manufacturing Rolls Royces for people who can only afford Ford Escorts.

In setting up a new business, the first thing is to convince your customers of the quality of your products and services. This can be inferred in all sorts of ways and long before a client sits in front of the mirror in your salon. There are lots of unspoken messages that will have been sent and received – the image of the business from the street, the quality of communication over the telephone, the decor and layout upon entry, and the courtesy and professionalism of reception. Once a level of quality has been achieved the most important thing is to maintain it. This factor is the hardest business aspect to control within a service industry.

In addition to the above topics you will need to set up your business systems. These can range from till procedures to filing, client care procedures, stock controls and so on. See pages 39–53 for more information.

financial forecasts and analysis

For a new business this can often be the most difficult part to develop. Your enthusiasm and optimism should reflect realistic business pressures. You will know what your overheads will be, but your income should be based upon your market research. The resultant figures from the cash flow forecast can then be translated into profit and loss and balance sheet forecasts.

set-up costs

Specify the amount and type of finance needed, and whether this will be by business overdraft, short-term

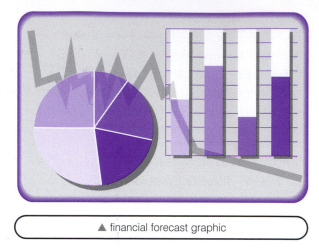

▲ financial forecast graphic

loans or longer-term arrangements. Don't forget to show how you intend to repay loans within your cash flow projections. Make sure that you apply for enough money at the outset; you don't want to be going backwards and forwards to the bank because of unrealistic forecasts.

overheads

When you show the bank manager your cash flow forecast, make sure that you have included the estimated costs of services, insurance, employee costs, interest, advertising costs etc.

Before a bank lends you any money it will want you to demonstrate your ability to repay the loan. When you're presenting your case, remember that you are the salesman for the project and the banker is the customer. Make sure you know your facts and figures. Keep in mind the targets you are trying to achieve and make sure you keep to your budget.

Although a bank will want to see your business plan if you want to borrow money, remember that the branch manager doesn't know everything. Ask yourself what they need to know in order to make a rapid decision in your favour. A well-completed business plan that demonstrates the applicant has a thorough understanding about their business project, matched with enthusiasm and a commitment to repay, will go a long way towards this outcome.

Make sure that your presentation is professionally documented and provide the manager with a copy that can be used to review the plan before committing the bank to any financial risk. If the manager comes back to you with questions, suggest revisions if necessary; a willingness and ability to modify the plan will show that you have been a thorough researcher who has made contingencies for such situations.

sales forecast

Much of the information supporting this aspect can be found elsewhere within this book. However, you will need to provide a sales forecast. So far you have explained what you are selling, where you are selling it and how you are going to sell it. Now you must indicate how much you are going to sell.

The sales forecast is the most important set of figures that you will have generated so far. These figures will be used to compile your cash flow, your profit and loss, and the balance sheet. These will, in turn, be used to calculate how much capital you need to get started, how much profit you expect to make and the long-term viability of the business.

appendices

This section should support your plan and give references to information used during its development. For instance, give examples of your market research and competitor analysis, and your job descriptions for key personnel. Stock and equipment brochures as well as substantiated costings are also needed.

the business premises

You will need to give size, situation and location details. Remember to include your professional costs in conveyancing or lease negotiation, as well as monthly repayments for mortgage or rentals for the property.

equipment

Identify your equipment requirements and types preferred. State the contractors who will be invited to supply you.

Your business plan will need to be written in a way that holds the interest of the reader. This can be difficult if you are not used to presenting written information. Always stick to the point; a prospective lender will soon tire of 'windy warm-ups'. Remember the level of readership – although you understand the technical terms used in your business, the reader might not and therefore fail to appreciate an important aspect of your plan.

■ starting a business? the basic facts

self-employed?

Self-employed people are those who work on their own for themselves, or in a partnership with one or more people. Inland Revenue consider an individual running his or her own shop as likely to be self-employed, whereas a worker engaged to assist in the shop is likely to be an employee.

As soon as you start a business in a self-employed capacity you have to inform:
■ the Inland Revenue (National Insurance Contributions (N.I.)) office
■ your local Tax office
■ H.M. Customs and Excise (if your taxable income is likely to be more than £51,000 in a twelve-month period) – see Part 4 on Managing VAT, pages 68–70.

New forms from Inland Revenue make this task easier and enable you to inform all of the above. The form CWF1 *Notification of Self-employment* will also register you for Class 2 (Self-Employed) National Insurance contributions. This form can be found in the back of Inland Revenue Publication *Starting your own business?* (CWL1) along with a form CA5601 which enables you to pay your class 2 NICs by Direct Debit.

income tax

The main tax that most people pay is income tax. This is charged on all types of earnings as well as investments. For each employee, the employer makes deductions for income tax, weekly or monthly, through the PAYE (Pay As You Earn) system. As a self-employed person however, you are responsible for paying your own tax. This is why you will need to keep full and accurate records relating to all your trading transactions (there are accounting differences for directors of companies). You will be required to make up the accounts (see pages 70–73) to the end of your first year's trading, the end of the calendar year, or the end of the tax year (5th April).

Tax calculations are made on trading profits for the accounting year which ends in the same tax year. This would mean that if your year end is made up to 31st October each year, the tax calculation for 2000/2001 will be based on your profits for the accounting year ending on 31st October 2000. Inland Revenue has a set system for tax calculation and for further information contact your local tax enquiry centre.

Each year in April you will receive a tax return. This will ask for all the information required to calculate your income tax. Normally, although you are responsible for the completion of the tax return, you would be best advised to pass this to your accountant for their assistance. The tax return also explains how the calculation for Class 4 NICs is made.

> **National Insurance Contributions affecting the self-employed**
>
> **Class 2 National Insurance Contributions are**
> - Flat rate payments (collected by Inland Revenue (N.I. Contributions))
>
> **Class 4 National Insurance Contributions are**
> - Profit related (and are based on the tax payer's own self-assessment at or above a set level)

You will need to save towards your tax liability. After your first year in self-employment you will be required to make two payments on account towards your tax bill each year, one on 31st January and the other on 31st July. A final payment of the balance of any tax due will be required on the following 31st January together with the first payment on account for the following tax year.

At the end of your year a set of formal accounts will be drawn up by your accountant. Formal accounts are usually in two parts (see year end accounts, pages 71–72):

1. The trading profit and loss account, a summary of the year's trading transactions
2. The balance sheet, showing the assets and liabilities of the business.

national insurance

Almost everybody who is in work has to pay NICs. The different types of contributions are divided into six classes. As referred to earlier in this chapter, the self-employed are liable to pay two classes – Class 2 and Class 4.

Class 2 contributions are a weekly flat rate payable to Inland Revenue (N.I. Contributions) office of £6.55 (for year 1999/2000). The Class 2 contribution is a personal liability, not a business liability, and therefore most self-employed people elect to pay them by direct debit. Class 2 NICs are due from the time you become self-employed and are payable continuously, except for complete weeks when you are ill.

Class 4 contributions are based on a percentage of your annual profits. The percentage may vary from year to year, or from government to government.

First steps as a new employer

Inland Revenue

Notification of Self Employment

Inland Revenue
HM Customs & Excise

When completed, return form to

Inland Revenue NI Contributions Office
Self Employment Directorate
Longbenton
Newcastle upon Tyne
NE98 1ZZ.

The Inland Revenue National Insurance Contributions Office will send a copy of the completed form to your Tax Office and Customs and Excise.

Use this form to tell the Inland Revenue and Customs and Excise that you have started self-employment.

It is not a Value Added Tax (VAT) registration form. If you think you are required, or need, to be registered for VAT please put a 'X' in this box.

For official use only

Yourself

Your title *(for example, Mr/ Mrs/ Miss/ Ms)* and current surname

Previous surname *(for example, your surname before you married)*

Your first name(s)

Your date of birth *(in figures)* — Day Month Year

Your home address

Postcode

Your home phone number *(include STD code)*

Your National Insurance number — Letters Numbers Numbers Numbers Letter

Women only - Your marital status – put 'X' in relevant box

Single Married Widowed Separated Divorced

If Married, Widowed or Divorced show date of event(s)
If more than one event, please prefix each event with either M, W or D.

Tax Office to which you sent your last Tax Return

Reference in that Tax Office

Your business

1 When did you start in business or when will you start? — Day Month Year

2 What sort of self employed work do you do / will you do?

If you are working in the fishing industry as a share fisherman put 'X' in this box

If you intend working as a subcontractor in the Construction Industry contact your Tax Office for a registration card application form.

CWF1(1999) BMSD2/99

Your business continued

3 What is your business name and address?

Postcode

Your business phone number *(include STD code)*

Your business fax number *(include STD code)*

4 What is your position in the business? *For example, owner, partner. If you are a subcontractor, put 'subcontractor'.*

5 Do you have any business partners?
Put 'X' in the relevant box No Yes
If you have answered 'No', please go to question 6.
If you have answered 'Yes', please state

Partner's full name

Partner's address

Postcode

His/her National Insurance number — Letters Numbers Numbers Numbers Letter
(if known)
If you have more than one partner, please give details on a separate sheet.

6 If you are unable to pay your Class 2 National Insurance contributions by Direct Debit, and would like further information about other payment arrangements, please put 'X' in the box

Do you want more information about exception from liability because of low earnings or deferment? If so, put 'X' in the relevant box
• exception from liability because of low earnings
• deferment (if you are both employed and self employed)

Please turn over

Inland Revenue

▲ form CWF1 notification of self-employment

However it currently stands at 6 per cent between a lower profit level of £7,530 and the upper profit level of £26,000 (1999/2000). These levels are based on your tax self-assessment in the same way as for Schedule D tax, and if payment is overdue it will be subject to interest.

employing others

When you take on employees you will need to tell your local tax office immediately. They will then send you a **New Employer's Starter Pack**. This pack contains instruction cards, ranges of tables and standard forms. As a new employer you will then be responsible for calculating your employees' wages, their tax as well as their NICs payable under the PAYE system. During the tax year you must:

- Deduct the correct amount of PAYE from your employees' pay
- Work out how much NICs you and your employees have to pay
- Keep a record of your employees' pay and the PAYE and NICs due
- Make monthly (or quarterly if PAYE and NICs amount to less than £600 per month) payments to the Inland Revenue accounts office.

At the end of the tax year you must:

- Send a return to the tax office showing the details of each employee's total pay, and the PAYE and NICs due
- Send details to the tax office about certain expenses you have paid to employees or benefits you have provided them with
- Give each employee who has paid PAYE and/or NICs and is still working for you at the end of the tax year, a certificate showing their pay, PAYE and NICs details
- Give your employees a copy of the information you have given the tax office about the expenses payments and benefits provided.

keeping records

Until recently there was no legal requirement to keep records for Inland Revenue, but the Self Assessment system has changed all that. Since April 1997 there has been a new system for making tax returns

Keeping records (brief summary)

For the purposes of Inland Revenue and/or H.M. Customs and Excise you must:

- keep accurate records of all your business transactions
- keep documents, i.e. receipts, invoices, bank statements and cheque stubs
- separate business transactions from personal finances
- keep your records available for a period of at least 5 years.

and paying tax, and this system has record-keeping requirements. These require you to:

- set up a system for keeping your tax records
- maintain the records throughout the year
- retain your records for as long as is necessary.

The rules say that, for business tax payers, 'the records required to be kept and preserved shall include' all the amounts received and expended in the course of trading and in the case of a trade involved in dealing in goods, all sales and purchases of goods made in the course of trading.

There is no prescriptive method for meeting these requirements, it is up to you to devise a system that is satisfactory. This will obviously depend on the size and type of business but should at least cover the following minimum requirements (extracted from *Self Assessment, a guide to keeping records for the self employed*). You will be expected to:

▲ keeping records

- Record all sales and other business receipts as they come in, and retain the records
- Keep back-up records, e.g. invoices, bank statements and paying-in slips to show where income came from
- Record all purchases and other expenses as they arise, and ensure that unless the amounts are very small, that you have and retain the invoices and/or receipts for them
- Keep a record of all purchases and sales of assets used in your business
- Record all the amounts taken out of the business bank account, or in cash, for you or your family's personal use
- Record all amounts paid into the business from personal funds, e.g. the proceeds of a life assurance policy.

examples of records

(Extracted from *Self Assessment, a guide to keeping records for the self employed*)

bank and building society accounts

You need to retain all bank and building society statements and pass books for any account into which any money from your business has been paid or credited, or out of which you have drawn any money for the business. If you do not have a separate business bank account, you need to keep a record of which transactions were personal, and which were business.

Unless your business is small or has few transactions, it would usually be helpful to maintain a separate bank account or accounts for the business.

stock and work in progress

At the end of your accounting year you should carry out a stocktaking exercise to identify the costs of your stock and/or work in progress, record the costs, and retain the records.

money from private sources used in your business

You should keep a record of any private money brought into the business, and where it came from (a legacy, a bank loan, or the proceeds from, for instance, a life assurance policy).

personal drawings

You should keep a record of any money you take for your own or your family's personal use from:

- business cash
- your business bank account or
- your personal bank account if you do not have a separate business bank account.

If you withdraw money by cheque, an entry on the cheque stub will be enough to show that this is for personal use.

payments to employees

If you are an employer you will also need to keep records to back-up any deduction in your accounts for wages, payments, benefits and such like, relating to your employees. You can get more advice on records and inspections in the *Employer's Further Guide to PAYE* (P7), *PAYE Inspections: Inspections of Employers' and Contractors' Records* (IR71) and *Code of Practice 3: Inspections of Employers' and Contractors' Records*.

record books

The most suitable types of books you should use to summarise all your business transactions will depend on the nature and size of your business. For most businesses it is good practice to keep during the year:

- a cash book (a summary and analysis of all bank account entries, or cash receipts, payments and drawings)
- a petty cash book, or some other simple record of your petty cash transactions.

If you run a larger business it may be useful for you to keep other account books as well. Your accountant – if you have one – can advise you on what extra books you should keep. If you do not have an accountant, you can ask your Tax Office for advice.

After the end of the year, you or your accountant may need to prepare other records to show how your business records have been used to arrive at the figures in your tax return.

Whatever record books you keep, you will find it easier if you write them up frequently. Amounts paid into or taken out of the petty cash should be recorded when the transaction goes through.

computer records

If you keep your records on a computer, you will still have to keep the original paper record of your sales, purchases and similar transactions, unless you use an optical imaging system or microfilm all your original documents.

common points of difficulty

1. Sales

Sales include:

goods taken from stock for your own or your family's consumption and not paid for in cash, and goods or services supplied to someone else in exchange for goods or services.

Even if you do not record these through a till, you will need to make a record at the time the transaction takes place of the goods taken or supplied and their retail selling price.

2. Expenditure without back-up evidence

All your expenditure should be backed-up by bills or other evidence, but if, exceptionally, you do not get a receipt for some small items of cash expenditure, such as taxi fares or tips, you should make a note as soon as you can of the amount you spent and what it was for.

3. Motor vehicles and other assets used for business and private purposes

If you use the same vehicle for both business and private purposes, you should keep enough details to enable you to split your total expenditure between business and private use. Usually it will be enough to keep a record of business and private mileage and split the vehicle

running costs in these proportions. There may be other assets which you use for both business and private purposes – for example, a house or shop premises which include a flat. If so, you will again need to keep sufficient records to work out what expenditure relates to business, and what to private use.

Here are some examples of records recommended for your type of business (retail shop). You should keep:

- till rolls or other form of electronic record of sales
- details of any other income, for example, National Lottery or football pools' commission

Self Assessment
A guide to keeping records for the self-employed

RECEIPTS

SA/BK3

Inland Revenue

Inland Revenue

▲ information booklets are obtainable from Inland Revenue (see appendix 2)

- a separate record of
  - any goods taken for your own or your family's personal use or provided in exchange for other goods or services;
  - any other items not rung through the till such as commission from football pools or dry cleaning, or rent from the flat above the shop;
  - any cash taken out of the till to pay small business expenses
- bills for purchases and expenses
- a record of stock on hand at the end of the year
- invoices
- all bank and building society statements, pass books, cheque stubs and paying-in slips which include details of business transactions (see page 13)
- cash book
- details of any private money brought into the business
- details of any money taken out of the business bank account or in cash for your own or your family's personal use
- details of any assets used for both business and private purposes.

■ leasing premises

What do you need to watch for when negotiating a lease?

A lease is a totally binding contract for the duration of the lease term. It will normally contain onerous clauses concerning responsibilities and liabilities. It is vitally important that a prospective tenant pays particular attention to the responsibilities concerning repairs and insurances.

Prospective tenants can often be so anxious to conclude the lease negotiations that important aspects such as these are overlooked, with devastating long-term effects. It is not until a demand from the landlord or managing agent arrives requesting substantial funds for carrying out repairs, that the problem is fully appreciated, by which time the tenant is legally committed.

lease pitfalls checklist

☑ Always ask for a summary of responsibilities from your solicitor, so that your surveyor can estimate your ongoing costs. If you are negotiating occupancy of part of an existing premises, you could find yourself likely to pay a percentage of total repairing costs which could perhaps extend to re-roofing the building, or even the installation of a new fire escape!

☑ Always obtain details of recent expenditure of building repairs and renovations from the landlord or managing agent, as this will provide some insight into cost implications.

☑ Always ask for the total cost of the building's insurance. This may be covered under a landlord's 'blanket' policy relating to numerous premises, some of which may have higher insurance values than your own, and therefore push up the costs.

taking up references

If you are starting out in business and looking to rent premises, you can be certain that you will be asked to provide references. Normally, references would be taken from your bankers and possibly two trading suppliers. This could prove particularly difficult if you have not yet started trading. In addition to this, you can expect a search to determine your creditworthiness. This information will be acquired from Credit Reference Agencies (see pages 18–19). These companies collect data about you from a variety of sources and provide it to interested parties at a fee.

So, at the very least you will be expected to provide bank references, but at all costs you should avoid giving personal guarantees, especially if this is linked to providing security such as your own home.

rent reviews

The 'tenant' should read the lease provisions regarding rent review very carefully. Often there are very strict provisions within the lease about the time-scale limits for responding to landlord rent review notices. Generally, rent review notices and quotes for new rentals are issued six months prior to the review date. Normally, rent review clauses written into leases state 'upward only reviews', which means that regardless of whether commercial property values have risen or fallen, you will be tied to increasing rental values. The common form of institutional lease is for a period of 25 years. The rental review period is sometimes nego-tiable; it can be every 5 years but more often than not it is every 3 years.

Rental increases are not necessarily automatic. Much depends on property values, availability of sites and local economics. Often the fair-minded owner will take this into account and defer such rental reviews.

fully repairing and insuring leases (FRIs)

The majority of all letting agreements comprise fully repairing and insuring leases. This means that the tenant is responsible for maintaining the property in good repair. The landlord will from time to time want to see that their investment is being properly maintained and will inspect the premises to ensure this. Visits by the landlord or agent usually take place on a yearly basis; you would not be expected to have disruptions to normal business at any other times.

■ want to buy a franchise?

Franchising is now appearing across all occupational sectors, from printing to pubs, burger premises to wedding organisers. This is a business trend that is continuing to expand.

In the current economic climate, franchising can be sometimes better protected from financial upheavals than the sole trader. The huge resources that a franchisor can bring into play far outweigh the efforts of the individual. The sole trader cannot match the expertise, marketing, training and promotional back-up offered by a proven franchisor.

However, this is not to say that franchising guarantees success. Banks and building societies have been known to get into trouble, and there have been some spectacular crashes with hairdressing franchise oper-ations in the past. Buying into a franchise operation is not a licence to print money. Things can go wrong,

franchisees have complained of incorrect accounts, calls not returned and help not readily given in difficult times. For those tempted by franchises – you need to be dedicated, to work hard over long hours and have your family's support.

The following information answers the most often asked questions, in an attempt to take the mystery out of franchising.

1. *What is a franchise?*
Very simply, it's the way for an individual – the franchisee – to run his or her own business under the name and proven format of an established company (the franchisor). In other words, it's a sort of business marriage.

2. *What are the benefits of a franchise?*
- You get to own a business without many of the problems that often occur when setting up on your own
- The business risk is less because the product has already been market tested and found to work
- You are involved with an established, recognised name
- Through the franchisor's support, you need less money to set up than if you were going it alone
- You will get a proven business package that will include training, help with advertising and promotions, and the benefits of bulk-buying.

3. *How much does it cost?*
The cost to the franchisees will vary according to the type and location of the premises. Generally, you will need an initial investment of between £10,000 to £100,000 to set up the business, followed by regular payments, based on turnover, as a form of royalties and possible management fees.

4. *As a franchisee, how soon will I see a profit?*
This depends on the individual and the economic climate. However, it's reasonable to expect a break-even figure at the end of two years.

5. *What can I expect for my money?*
When you 'buy' a franchise, you get an array of already-established services. While packages vary according to the company, you can expect:
- to be your own boss
- corporate identity

- use of a well-known name
- help with management and accounts, plus plenty of informed advice on running the business
- ongoing staff training
- backing for marketing, advertising and promotion
- bulk-buying of stock.

You can also expect help with:
- picking a site
- the design of the salon and fitting it out
- getting planning permission
- advice on raising the money.

6. *How do I go about raising the money?*
First make sure you have enough money to buy the franchise and that you don't over-commit yourself. Then, you need to convince your bank manager you are a sound bet. Bits of paper, vague questions and woolly answers are not the way to go about it. Before you approach the bank, you should sit down and draw up a proper business plan (see The business plan, pages 4–9).

Most banks have helpful leaflets on franchising and how to go about raising money, as well as specialist franchise managers. If in doubt, ask.

7. *What should I check out before I sign?*
- Look at as many franchise operations within the hairdressing industry as you can
- Check out the company you choose thoroughly, particularly how sound it is, before becoming involved. And what's its track-record? Rapid growth is not necessarily a good thing as it can mean a company's resources are stretched
- How long has the company been in business? The best answer is several years, with a number of franchises successfully up and running
- If it's a new franchise, make sure a 12-month pilot scheme was operated with audited accounts available
- Get a complete list of existing franchises, and ring up as many as possible and check how well they are doing
- Are you going to be the company's only salon in the area? You don't want the franchisor to have another just up the road
- What's the true cost of buying the franchise? Get the franchisor to give you a complete statement of all costs

involved in buying, opening and operating a franchised outlet. And it should include an overview of all these factors or you could be buying into an undercapitalised venture

- What are your rights to renew or extend the contract beyond its original term?
- What happens if you want to sell or transfer the ownership of the franchise?
- Under what terms and conditions can you end the contract?
- Always take professional advice from a solicitor, bank and accountant – and make sure they are familiar with franchising
- And read the small print.

■ is my credit good?

Having a good credit track-record means everything today. You can no longer expect to borrow money without one, in fact many suppliers will refuse to trade with you unless your credit scoring comes up to scratch. Credit scoring is the preferred route nowadays for extending credit to an individual. When you apply for a loan or overdraft, or even supply of utilities, your details and financial history will be made available via the Credit Reference Agencies (CRAs).

So what information do they hold? Credit reference agencies such as Experion and Equifax are large data bureaux. These agencies obtain information about you and sell it to interested parties. They acquire information from a variety of sources:

electoral roll

If you pay community charge and are entitled to vote you will be on your local authority's electoral roll.

address

Your address is confirmed by the electoral roll and billing from utilities, i.e. water companies, electricity companies, telecommunications companies and such like.

credit and charge cards

If you have any credit or charge cards, your account history and status (your payment record) will be held by the CRAs.

County Court Judgements (CCJs)

If you have been unable to pay a bill (particularly a utilities bill from the firms stated above), regardless how small, you can expect to receive a summons for non-payment. Unless the bill is settled a court judgement will be made against you. This is called a CCJ (County Court Judgement). This is bad news; should you then (within 6 years) apply for loans, credit, mortgages or any form of borrowing, you can expect to be refused! If settlement is made at some later date, you can apply for a Certificate of Satisfaction proving that the debt has been fully repaid. You can then write to the individual CRAs and request that a notice of correction is applied to your file.

bankruptcy

If you have ever been declared bankrupt while self-employed or within a partnership in business that has failed, the CRAs will hold this information on file. Unfortunately, even if a Bankruptcy Order has been made against you and three years later a Certificate of Discharge is applied for (new legislation is attempting to reduce the 3-year discharge to 6 months), the information relating to the bankruptcy will still be held on file for 6 years. A discharged bankrupt has little more credibility with lenders than one who has not been discharged.

can I see my credit file?

Yes. Anyone has the right to see exactly what is held on file against them. You can obtain a booklet *You and Your Credit File* from Equifax Europe (UK) Limited, Department 2E, PO Box 3001, Glasgow G81 2DT (telephone: 0990 143700). This will explain how you contact a CRA to either view or correct your file.

your rights under the Consumer Credit Act 1974

If you think that anything in the credit reference agency's file is wrong, and that you are likely to suffer as a result, your rights are protected under the Consumer Credit Act 1974.

your rights if an entry is wrong

If you think that anything in the file is wrong and you are likely to suffer as a result, you have the following rights:

- If you think that there is no basis at all for the entry, you may write to the agency requesting it to remove the entry
- If the entry is incorrect, you may write to the agency requesting it to remove or amend the entry. When writing to the agency, you should say why you think that the entry is incorrect.

Within 28 days of receiving your letter the agency should write and tell you that it has removed the entry from the file, or amended it, or taken no action. If the entry has been amended, the agency must send you a copy of the amended entry.

If the agency tells you that it has taken no action, or if it does not reply to your letter within the 28 days, or if it makes an amendment that you think is unsatisfactory, you may write a note correcting the entry and send it to the agency with a letter requiring the agency to add the note to its file about you and to include a copy of it when furnishing information included in or based on the entry which it corrects.

Your *Notice of Correction* should give a clear and accurate explanation of why you consider the entry to be incorrect. It must not be more than 200 words long. You can prepare the note yourself or with the help of, for example, a citizens advice bureau, a consumer advice centre or a solicitor. If however the agency considers that your *Notice of Correction* is incorrect, defamatory, frivolous, scandalous, or unsuitable for any other reason, it can ask the Director General of Fair Trading to give a ruling as to what it must do.

timing conditions

- If the agency has replied to the first letter in which you objected to the entry, you must send your *Notice of Correction* within 28 days of receiving its reply
- If the agency did not reply to your first letter within 28 days, your *Notice of Correction* must be sent within the next 28 days

- If the agency accepts your *Notice of Correction* (i.e. it does not seek a ruling from the Director General of Fair Trading), it must tell you within 28 days that it intends to comply with your request.

If you want any further details about your rights under the Consumer Credit Act, or about the time-scales within which Credit Reference Agencies must deal with your queries, you can obtain a booklet, *No Credit?*, from Eros, PO Box 2, Central Way, Feltham, Middlesex, TW14 0TG.

Advice about how to deal with your debts is also available from a number of independent organisations:

- your local Citizens Advice Bureau
- Consumer Credit Counselling Service (telephone: 0345 697301)
- National Debt Line Service (telephone: 0121 359 8501).

◼ salon refit?

how often should you refit?

This depends on how fashion-conscious and budget-conscious you are. At the very least you'll have to freshen the place up with a lick of paint every couple of years. As a general rule, salons should be refitted every five or seven years, and given a full face-lift every seven to ten years.

how much should you spend?

Your outlay will vary according to the extent of the work, the size of your salon and its location. Innovia Design suggests anywhere between £5,000 and £125,000. A full design management and fitting package for a salon with nine styling positions and three backwashes will cost £44,000 to £55,000.

Always look beneath the veneer when considering quotes. You may budget to replace a floor, only to find the joists are rotten when you look underneath it.

where do you start?

- The view of the shop front is what your clients and potential clients see first. So this has to be of prime importance

GROUND FLOOR PLAN

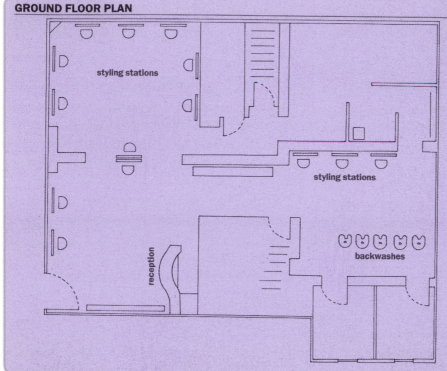

styling stations

styling stations

reception

backwashes

- How you display your products is vital. The retail and reception area has to make an impact
- Updated and improved lighting dramatically improves any salon and doesn't affect planning restrictions. When looking at colour schemes, your ceiling, walls and floor should emerge with clean lines in basic colour schemes
- Styling chairs, units and mirrors can be changed according to their condition. A fresh, modern interior will keep staff morale up.

themed surroundings

Try to keep your designs simple: the more involved the interior, the higher the proportional cost.

Classic lines tend not to date as quickly as themed interiors and are often cheaper to replace. Look at other salons and see how different firms create their own 'corporate image'.

general tips for salon design
reception

Retailing is changing fast and so are the aspirations of your clients. Change seems to be the buzzword so keep things flexible. Manufacturers are bringing out new lines all the time, so you need to bear this in mind when designing your reception.

backwashes

'White is right' ceramics need to look clean and inviting. Steer clear of coloured basins as they can look dirtier more quickly. Steel and chrome fittings should sparkle and gleam, and remember your water system should be able to deliver lots of both *hot* and cold water.

Mahogany

Mahogany

workstations

The salon is a place of luxury and should have a 'feel good' factor. This can only be experienced when adequate room is provided between styling positions. Both clients and staff need room in order to be comfortable. Minimum chair centres should not be less than 1.3 metres, and from the mirror backwards, including sufficient styling manoeuvrability, should be at least 2 metres.

floors

Wood may be durable but is apparently on the way out. Ceramic tiles can be beautiful but tile grouting can harbour dirt. Therefore, salons need easy-to-clean floor coverings and this is best provided by sheet vinyl coverings. These can be relatively inexpensive, or a 'leg and arm' job.

staff areas

Staff room accommodation is often left out of the budget. Ask your Rep. It is a very important part of the overall salon success. Staff need a clean comfortable area where, at times, a little respite and relaxation can be provided.

what colour?

Colour can transform a salon interior, so selecting the right shade is essential. If you have a certain ambience or theme in mind, choosing the correct colour will help to 'cement' that image. The use of yellows and blues can create a holiday atmosphere in the salon, which assimilates the blue associated with sky and the yellow of sand.

Generally, blue and green shades are regarded as 'cool tones' and these are relaxing. Yellow is thought to be a cheerful sunny colour and the red and orange tones are described as 'warm tones'. However, the degree of darkness or lightness of a colour will change its mood. For example, a highly saturated Mediterranean blue conveys activity, whereas a darker shade of the same hue can appear passive.

Different colours mean different things to different people. Care should be taken before choosing colours for your salon. You need to consider the age of the target clientele first of all. The use of strong vivid colours much appreciated by teenagers may be considered brash and naive by a more discerning older clientele.

Whatever the colour scheme in your salon, it has to be complemented by the correct lighting. For example, if orange walls are illuminated by strong white halogen lights, they will reflect colour from the walls on to other surfaces. Conversely, the same orange walls illuminated by fluorescent lights will appear browner. It is important to remember that the colour on salon walls will reflect off the mirrors on to your clients' faces and hair. Green walls, for example, will throw an ashen hue on to your clients' faces, making them appear quite pale and sick!

Getting the colour right can go a long way towards enhancing an 'architecturally imperfect' interior. Darker tones have the ability to disguise a 'lumpy' wall surface. If you are working to a tight budget, don't invest too heavily on expensive wall finishes, often cheaper solutions such as emulsion can be quite adequate. If you don't like them, then they are easily changed. Salons are working environments, so materials and finishes must be able to withstand the day-to-day splashes and spills. Find out if there is a simple way to seal those surfaces that doesn't cost the earth.

classic versus contemporary

Fashions come and go but the classics always remain. There are two different standpoints to the approach to interior design. Currently, salons seem to be opting for either the safer classic interiors involving the usage of neutral colours, creams and so on, or on the other hand the use of terracotta, yellow and powder blues seems strong in the fashion stakes.

The 1990s colour fashions have left their mark on salon interior design. You may remember the late 1970s and early 1980s 'if it's wood it must be good' theme. Every salon seemed to find diverse uses for strange pieces of pine furniture. In fact, salons became alternative showrooms for 'nearly antiques shops'. Now things are different, the 'one off' artistic salon environment utilises the popular paint effects, metal furniture and etched glass, whilst the larger salon groups go for the safer neutral looks. Your salon's look will define your public image, and who knows, anyway, what's around the corner?

■ time management

We could think that, as hairdressers, we are good managers of time, particularly when our whole working life has to run to time. However the manager's work does not stop there.

Running a salon involves many different tasks: working with clients, ordering stock, book-keeping and accounts, handling staff and keeping everyone happy. How do you make time for all this and be a good manager into the bargain?

How can you expect to manage anyone else if you cannot manage yourself? Being disorganised is like a virus that will spread to others. If you're always in complete turmoil, your staff will be affected in the same way, and this in turn will affect clients. This ever-decreasing spiral will, in the end, lead to your own ever-increasing stress levels.

▲ time management

get organised

If you don't take control and organise your time, you'll never have the time for anything. After people, time is the most important asset to your business, so it must be managed well. You have to take control of the time at your disposal and decide how you want to spend it.

prioritise things to do

Tasks need to be graded in order of urgency. Don't waste time dealing with non-urgent tasks. First of all make a list of things to do. Once you have a complete list of everything to do, you can set about prioritising the content. The list could then be tabulated to cover things to do today, this week and this month (see below).

Lists are the most important time management tools, but they only work if you stick with them religiously. Find a system that works for you and a way of

Things to do today	Things to do this week	Things to do this month

keeping your list at hand so you can work with it, add to it and, finally, cross things off it.

Write things down – people are neither computers nor infallible. If you don't write things down you may forget some of them, only remembering them at the last minute or too late. Make list-writing your daily habit and set aside time to review the items on your lists on a regular basis.

The quotation 'never handle a piece of paper more than once' should be remembered. Attend to those important issues as soon as possible, we could all spend our lives putting things off until tomorrow. If we get those annoying little things done straightaway, we could save so much time.

People who really are in control of their time plan their activities, remembering that social and leisure time is just as important as their business life.

■ stress management

There is an old saying 'hard work never killed any-body'. Maybe the wise sages who originated this say-ing related hard work to hard labour and general tiredness. These days 'hard work' implies much, much more. Hard work, or putting it into today's terms, hard work and stress, is a killer! The obsession with work can wreck your health, happiness and relationships.

At the time of writing this book, 'it's official', the British work longer hours than any other nation in the European Union. So what's wrong with working long hours? Nothing, provided that you can stand the pace. Many have had to; they have become acclimatised to working longer and longer. Corporate 'downsizing' has led to fewer staff having to cope with increasing work loads, staff considered lucky to still have a job.

The downside of this is increasing tiredness, irri-tability and a shifting emphasis from personal goals to the work itself – hence cometh the 'workaholic'. This condition is best described as a compulsive devotion to work at the expense of all else. A workaholic puts in extended hours, has an inability to say 'no' and finds delegation difficult. The poor individual feels con-stantly time driven, always rushing from task to task and is unsuccessful because of trying to do too many things at once. In many cases normal sleep patterns are disrupted, sex drive and energy diminish, and there is increasing dependence on caffeine, alcohol, smoking and other stimulants.

There are enough stresses in life anyway without making things worse:

- Personal crises
- Money concerns
- Family needs
- Health concerns.

If you want to avoid the psychiatrist's couch you will need to take control of your life, find time for relaxation, moderate excesses, maintain social relationships and take regular exercise.

▲ stress management

2 principles of marketing

part 2

principles of
marketing

■ marketing

What is a 'market'? A market can be simply described as a group of people able and willing to buy a particular product or service. The activities involved in 'reaching' this particular group are called marketing. The collection of information and the analysis of data are market research.

Market research is essential in order to gain a thorough knowledge of your customers and competitors.

Whatever your talents are as a skilled hairdresser, you must not lose sight of the fact that no customers mean no business. You may have the idea that lots of people out there need your skills, but unless you can reach them you will not be able to pay the rent or repay the bank its money.

You can make an assessment of your understanding of whether the customers exist by answering the following questions:

How many potential customers are there for my business?
How many are there in reality?
Who are my customers?
Where are my customers?
Why should they want my salon's services?
Who do they go to at the moment?
How much will they pay ?
How often will they come back?
Who else can provide these services?
How strong is the competition?

In planning your business, do nothing until you can answer these questions. This seems like a harsh statement but it is vitally important. The collection of information needed to answer these questions may be derived from a number of marketing sources, i.e. you must assemble market information.

market information

During the preparation of a business start-up it is easy to overlook the opportunity to check already published information, much of which is freely available and easily accessible. The most obvious place to start assessing your market size, trends, pricing and competitors is via your local library or the Internet.

Customers	Current (if applicable) Potential (the ones you seek to develop)
Suppliers	Wholesalers, manufacturer representatives, franchises
Competitors	Local direct competition
Trade associations	HMWA, NHF, Incorporated Guild of Hairdressers etc.
Regional bodies	Business Link/Local Training and Enterprise Councils
Publications	Specialist magazines, newspapers, business/telephone directories
The firm	In-house reports and collected data
Official statistics	Listed below
The Internet	A global information resource

▲ sources of information

Other sources of information could be:

- County, borough and town profiles (county and district councils)
- Census of Population (HMSO)
- Family Expenditure Survey (HMSO)
- Mintel Market Intelligence
- Regional Trends (HMSO).

For businesses already up and running, much of your planning information will come from internal sources. More often than not, it is the internal sources that provide the best data for analysis as such data will be based upon past results, promotional success, forecasts and previous business activities. These not only provide historically based information for forecasting but are useful in achieving more effective control of ongoing operations. The following principle, identified by Michael E. Porter, indicates the five forces acting upon a business:

- The power of competitors
- The power of buyers in the market
- The power of suppliers to the business
- The threats posed by potential entrants
- The threats posed by substitute products.

You need to put your services and products to the test, so this will mean making comparisons between yourself and the competition. This next section encourages you to make those comparisons.

competitor comparison

Service attributes	Worse −3 −2 −1	Same	Better +1 +2 +3	How vital is this attribute? Is it essential, preferred or other?
Service availability				
Range of services/treatments				
Ranges of products used/sold				
Communication/helpfulness				
Presentation/appearance				
Quality of work output				
Home care and advice				
Consultation				
Time allowed and taken				
Refreshments				
Methods of payment				
Image				

consumer research

In an existing business situation you already have a client base. Putting your business to the test is the only proactive way of finding out if you are meeting your clients' needs. The easiest way of sampling opinion is through a client satisfaction survey. In situations where it is possible for questionnaires to be discreetly completed on the premises, the validity of such materials weighs very heavily indeed. Conversely, if the decision is taken for clients to fill in questionnaires some later time at home, insufficient data may be returned for a true analysis to be conducted.

Devising a client satisfaction survey, or any other survey for that matter, is a difficult task since we might try to build in too much data in order to get a 'focused' analysis.

A major national survey was conducted during the mid 1990s by the consumers' defender *WHICH?* magazine. This survey simply set out to identify what customers expected within their service at the hairdressers. From 2000 questionnaires sent out, 50 per cent were returned (not a bad hit rate). One in ten of those people was appalled that they were charged extra for refreshments. Hairdressers be warned! If this is indicative of the nation as a whole, we can see that what may be considered as just a small incidental charge, may be a critical influencing factor to customers and therefore to business success.

The Good Salon Guide is a sort of marketing group for hairdressing, This company will, if requested, verify a salon's quality rating matched against specific criteria. Salons applying for 1, 2, 3, 4 or 5 star ratings need to demonstrate their ability in meeting their requirements. Obviously, different ratings are awarded in respect of staff expertise and knowledge, salon profile, facilities and related aspects, but built into these criteria are also the simple expectations of new magazines, tea, coffee and adequate 'loos'. From these considerations it is obvious that our clients expect a comprehensive service, 'frills and all'.

When you devise a survey for your clients, regardless of whether you are sampling service quality or client expectation, always aim to keep the possible responses indicative and objective. 'Fuzzy' subjective data is of little use. You need to be able to identify:

- Levels of service quality
- Standards of communication
- Clients' expectations
- Shortfalls in provision
- Possible areas for improvements.

When the specific questions have been selected, a scaling of response should be introduced (see below):

Very poor		Average		Very Good
1	2	3	4	5

It is better to gauge a 'feel' of the level of approval or dislike than just to expect a 'yes' or 'no' response.

who are your customers?

What type of clients do we have, and where do they come from? If a hundred hairdressers were asked who their customers were and why they had chosen each individual hairdresser, there would be a variety of answers. Conversely, if the clients of those hundred hairdressers were asked why they visited a particular hairdresser, even more divergent replies would come out.

The answers would range from the physiological to the psychological, sociological and possibly the geographical. All this technicality does not make the reasons any easier to understand. The customer might even like the way that X does her hair! This statement does seem a bit obvious, but it is also based on 25 years' experience. We want clients to come to our salons because they like and appreciate what we do and are willing to pay our price for it.

In the next example I have borrowed an illustration that shows the life cycle of a manufactured product. What parallels, if any, to hairdressing do you see?

In this example we see clearly defined phases within a product's 'life', starting from the development and introduction phases, proceeding to a more active and prosperous growth phase, then the maturity and saturation phases, and finally a decline. We can assume that the profitability curve will mirror this one.

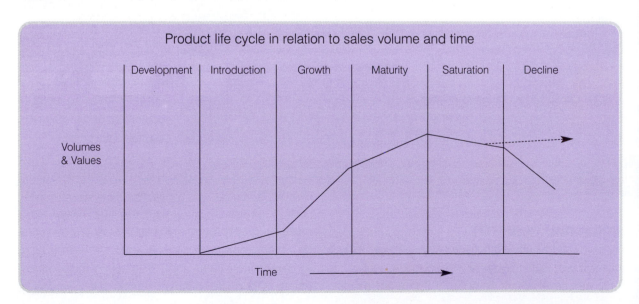

Product life cycle in relation to sales volume and time

Development | Introduction | Growth | Maturity | Saturation | Decline

Volumes & Values

Time

Often manufactured products are involved in revamping, repackaging and possibly a re-launch within their saturation phase. This regeneration 'reboots' the product's life and defers the decline stage to some future point beyond the foreseeable horizon.

To me, this product life analogy seems to mirror the hairdressing business. To prolong the stage where profits are maximised, so fresh, new ideas, services and treatments need to be introduced in order that the salon's profitable life is extended.

During the 'life' of the salon, we see the initial interest, excitement, wonder and exclusivity that is created when a new salon first opens. The strong growth phase occurs when we have a motivated staff and good reputation. This in turn leads to a 'boom time' when the returns of hard work, investment in people and training pay off. And, finally, if continued impetus, support and encouragement are not maintained, boredom unfortunately sets in. The salon is then vulnerable to potential staff loss, lack of continued motivation and inevitable downturn!

Marketing research has shown that future clients' needs will change; recent publications showing future trends indicate that salons should be seeking to broaden and extend their existing services to cover a variety of additional services, such as:

- Nail services
- Aromatherapy
- Massage techniques
- Retailing/merchandising, and even
- Image consultancy.

Unless we maintain a strong ongoing client base which responds to and changes with our clients' needs, we will reach decline all too soon!

◼ market strategy for new business

What is your market strategy? How do you see your new business as a service provider? How will your firm achieve success? Which of the following statements best suits your aims? We aim to:

- Provide basic services to clients at a low cost
- Provide unique services to clients at a high cost
- Provide services to specific client types.

As soon as we start to think more deeply about these different aims, we are already beginning to analyse the strategy of our business. We are starting to make decisions about the services that we will offer, the costs that we will charge, the type of customers that we aim to serve.

price leadership

This means becoming a low-cost service provider and is essentially a numbers game, i.e. 'putting bums on seats'. It is a 'no frills' standard service approach. Price leadership means providing your services more cheaply than your competitors do, and creates a strong message in market strategy. As profits are generated by volume considerations, you will need to be careful about the implementation:

1. *Time* – keep a close check on timings, such as the 15-minute cut only, or the 30-minute cut and finish
2. *Services* – limit the variety of services available to, say, the cut, or the cut and finish; maximise your profits by minimising the standards of service quality
3. *Consultation* – standardise the consultation process so that a simple series of steps can be followed
4. *Cost minimisation* – keep your costs low by controlling stock wastage, purchases and support staff to stylists.

Price leadership is an effective strategy for penetrating new market areas; or, if you are a new salon in the area, it will attract the price-conscious or those in changed circumstances, such as people with young families or on low incomes.

unique or specialist strategy

This approach means that the salon sets out to be unique within its area of expertise, or provides benefits which are valued by clients. This degree of uniqueness or specialism will normally attract a high price. Salons that adhere to this strategy will provide services not currently on offer anywhere else. If you wish to take this angle within your marketing, compare your strengths and weaknesses against your competitors and maximise on those services which are your strengths. These could be:

- Specialist or creative colouring
- Long hair techniques
- Hair extensions
- Total service from consultation to finished effect.

focused strategy

This principle is based upon taking the competitive edge within a specific market group and meeting their needs. In situations where salons try to be all things to all people, there is a danger that potential customers do not know that the salon caters for their particular needs.

Often, there are conflicts between different market segments, so you should be careful if you aim to take this approach. For example, if you set out to develop a strong student contingent and cater for their tastes, which may include music, ambience, decor etc., you may find that this deters the older clientele.

If you do want to develop specific market segments:

1. Decide which ones will be compatible
2. Establish the existing proportions of different segments within the client base
3. Identify the needs of those clients falling into specific client groups
4. Develop a focused marketing campaign aimed at reaching the particular target group.

■ market strategy for an existing business

For businesses already up and running, their future strategy may be better categorised within one of the following statements:

market retention

We will concentrate on providing existing clients with services, treatments and products by using our staff's expertise and knowledge which will give us the competitive edge.

market expansion option 1

We will expand our business by offering our existing services, treatments and products to new types of customers.

market expansion option 2

We will expand our business by offering new services, treatments and products to our existing clients.

diversification

We will expand our business by moving into another type of service area.

These four market strategies are very different and each have varying levels of risk! The market retention strategy carries the lowest risk. The second strategy, market expansion option 1, carries a higher risk. This strategy benefits from delivering existing service and skills but to new market groups. This could be via a new salon, or to new client groups such as children or students, or even via a mobile service, say for weddings. The third strategy, market expansion option 2, would carry a slightly higher risk also. In this situation the firm looks to expand by offering new services, treatments etc. to existing clients. This can be risky unless you know your clients well. For example, is there any point in spending large sums on training and set-up costs for hair extensions if your existing clients are on average 50+. The fourth strategy, diversification, is high risk. It is often considered by hairdressers as a logical option, particularly when existing and available space can be turned into a new use – that beauty salon you've always wanted upstairs, or the coffee shop downstairs. The problem with these new ventures is that they don't always enhance the existing firm; your customers may not approve of the new corporate direction, or you may generate custom from conflicting market segments.

■ market segmentation

Market segmentation tries to determine the differences between potential buyers; this refers to their buying habits, buying patterns and preferences. Everyone is different and so are their specific needs. We have already stated that salons cannot be all things to all people. So in marketing speak, total markets should be divided so as to identify dissimilarity between segments and similarity within each segment. In other words we look at people as a whole, define the specific types or groups, and then find the needs and wants of those within specific groups.

The specific groups, i.e. market segmentation variables, are detailed below:

Age, Sex, Family size, Income, Occupation, Education	Demographic segments
Urban, Rural, Density of population	Geographic segments
Lifestyle, Personality, Attitudes	Psychographic segments
Religion, Race, Social class	Sociocultural characteristics

Having focused on a particular client group, how do the aspects and attributes of your services relate to clients' preferences, and how does interest in these aspects and attributes lead to a buying decision?

- What does the client buy, i.e. what type of service or product?
- When does the client buy, i.e. how often?
- Why does the client buy, i.e. for cheapness, loyalty, quality or accessibility?
- What is the mode of buying, i.e. walk-in, by telephone or regular standing appointment?

evaluating market segments

It is obvious that a well-managed business keeps close track of their turnover and profits etc., but what about future trends?

Business success is what we all want, but how do we know what works and what doesn't?

You may think that as long as the business is doing well this doesn't really matter. But it does. We need to know what aspects of the business have worked in the past, in order to plan objectively for the future. The aspects referred to could be a number of different things, as covered elsewhere in this book, such as productivity, efficiency, purchasing, time management or financial control. However, none of these is more important than understanding what has satisfied our customers in the past, and *will continue* to do so in the future.

how do we plot the future within the various market segments?

We can use simple illustrations to monitor our progress. For instance, Service group by Total custom:

Clients → Services ↓	Students	Working females up to 50 years old	Non–working females up to 50 years old	Other females	TOTALS
Cutting only					
Cut and finish					
Colouring					
Perming					

This can be adapted to cover any market segment, service or treatment.

Students only → Colouring ↓	Last quarter sales	Current quarter sales	Next quarter's sales	Trend (± per cent)
Full head colour				
Lightening				
High-lighting				
Roots only				

■ the marketing mix

The marketing mix or 4 P's as it is often referred to, is probably the hardest of all marketing concepts to grasp. But in the context of understanding your own business it will seem quite straightforward, and in this sense that is just what it is. If you think of your business as an entity that exists in a competitive environment, it must compete to exist. Therefore, somewhere along the line your handling of:

■ Price

■ Place

■ Product

■ Promotion

must be working! These four business aspects, or shall we say variables, are intrinsic to your success.

In a way it's like a favourite recipe. Imagine preparing your favourite recipe for dinner with friends:

Your Favourite Recipe!	
1. Have you got all the necessary ingredients?	✓
2. Have you measured out the right amounts?	✓
3. Have you blended the ingredients together?	✓
4. Have you added the herbs and spices?	✓
5. Have you cooked it for the right length of time?	✓
6. Does the finished dish look good?	✓
7. Does it smell good?	✓
8. Now see if your guests think it tastes good!	✓

Then, taking just one group, we can analyse Service by Segment:

The above illustration is just a simple analogy of something that is very important. When all the research, planning, analysis etc. is over, you will have created an image of your business for your potential customers – an image that can finally be sampled, or to put it another way, 'experienced' by the senses of your clients.

■ SWOT analysis

SWOT analysis is the business tool for your strategic planning and subsequent setting of objectives. The study of the business *Strengths*, *Weaknesses*, *Opportunities* and *Threats* should be undertaken in order to devise a detailed plan of action.

This is undertaken in three different stages:

1. Looking internally at the business and deciding its strengths and weaknesses
2. Looking externally outside the business and selecting the alternatives which present the best opportunities whilst avoiding the greatest threats
3. Then, finally, based on the earlier decisions, developing action plans to cover short-, medium- and long-term objectives.

SWOT analysis

Start your
SWOT analysis
by jotting down
on a piece of
paper the main
headings and
list the attributes
and aspects
which affect the
business.

Strengths	Weaknesses
Opportunities	Threats

pricing

Pricing, that is setting the selling price, is a complex procedure with many implications. From a marketing standpoint it could have a critical impact on how a service or product is perceived. At one end of the scale it can convey inferences of luxury or premium quality; whereas, at the other, it may be perceived as cheap, inferior or nasty.

So where do you pitch your pricing levels? There is always the temptation to establish your pricing based upon the internal costs of the business. This is only half the story, since it is impossible to set prices without calculating your expected income set against those costs. The successful business will:

- Research other competitors' prices within its market area
- Remember that price is an attribute of the market and the service

- Assess other factors in relation to competition, such as service quality and added value
- Assess its own costs
- Realise that it is easier to reduce prices than to put them up.

break-even

To set your prices accurately you need to be aware of some basic calculations and terms.

Gross sales: total sales derived from services and treatments, i.e. numbers sold (N) × unit prices (P)
Fixed costs: those relating to rent, rates, water and so on (F)
Variable costs: those relating to consumables, staff etc. (V)
Selling price (P)
Contribution: the selling price minus the variable costs

So taking the above:

Total sales revenue (R) is $R = (N \times P)$
Contribution is $C = (P - V)$
Therefore total costs are $TC = F + (N \times V)$
Since break-even occurs when Total sales and Total costs are equal, we find that

$$(N \times P) = F + (N \times V)$$

If we divide each side by N we find that the price needed (P) in order to break-even on sales volumes of services and treatments (N) is given by

$$P = \frac{F}{N} + V$$

or conversely the number of sales required to break-even at price P can be shown to be

$$N = \frac{F}{P - V}$$

These formulas assume that you have already calculated your fixed and variable costs, or have previous firms' accounts to work from. If you haven't any figures to work from, then you will need to calculate your own contribution costs.

contribution costs

Contribution is the term used and favoured in accountancy where there is a wide range of products or services, and within which there are difficulties in allocating the overheads. Quite simply, taking the range of services available within the salon, such as cut and finish or perming, and trying to work out the different unit costs can be a difficult task.

So, in working out contribution we need to know the proportion of wages (including employer's NIC), as well as the cost of consumables (goods, beverages, laundry, water etc.).

In making these calculations, let's take the salon service of a cut and finish. We take this service because it provides a good indicator of the business, because the main bulk of work carried out within the salon will be your bread and butter service, i.e. cut and dry. And it is from this service pricing that you must achieve your profit margins.

If you look at your monthly sales figure and divide this by the number of customers, you will arrive at an average figure. For example, suppose the salon turnover in one month is £11,000 and the number of customers is 560. The average billing is £11,000 divided by 560 = £19.64.

As a rule of thumb, if the average figure works out to be less than the average price of a cut and blow, then you may be losing money; if it's more, you're in the 'black'.

Taking the figure of £19.64, we can work out the contribution to the firm. First remove the VAT portion:

$$£19.64 \times 7 \text{ divide by } 47 = £2.93$$

so £19.64 − £2.93 = £16.71.

A cut and blow takes 45 minutes and staff salary is £12,500 per annum + 15 per cent commission. We need to know the salary per appointment slot – 12,500 divided by, say, 48 weeks (with due allowance for holidays):

12,500/48 = £260.42 + average commission of 15 per cent = £299.48

£299.48/40 hours = £7.49 per hour × 75 per cent (to work out cost of 45 minutes)

$$£7.49 \times 75 \text{ per cent} = £5.62$$

This is then added to the other variable costs: £2.45 (for materials etc.). This gives

$$£5.62 + £2.45 = £8.07 \text{ costs}$$

Removing the costs from the net figure, we get £16.71 − £8.07 = £8.64. This contribution of £8.64, i.e. the gross profit margin before operating expenses, represents 52 per cent of the net figure. See pages 70–74 for explanation of the Balance Sheet.

■ marketing opportunities through information technology

Your existing salon clients provide the greatest potential for increases in the levels of future business. The advent of store loyalty cards is probably the best example of market opportunities developed through Information Technology (IT) management today. In this situation a store or supermarket provides an incentive to the 'shopper' to apply for a loyalty card; this can be by offering a discount or money off, depending on how much is spent. In applying to the store for this card, personal information such as name, address, post code etc. is given. This information is then held within a database.

Over a period of time, patterns will develop as the buying habits are monitored. This will occur when purchases are made and the card is prompted for and 'swiped' through the till. Let's say that within a basket of shopping there are some baby foods and sterilising materials. This would indicate to the data manager that a young child is either present or expected. This information could then be passed or sold to a third party along with other similar identified customers, who just happen to receive a mother-and-baby mail-order catalogue in the post.

The patterns created by your customers are vitally important to your business. The market information tables below identify some of the data types that can be managed to provide important market information:

About clients	Types of data for retrieval and analysis
Where do they come from?	Do you fare better in some areas than in others?
How often do they visit the salon?	Monthly, six-weekly, quarterly?
What type of client does your salon attract?	Professional, married with children, retired with high disposable income, students?
How do they find you?	Referral, promotions, displays, advertising?
Which stylist do they go to?	Always the same one or different ones?
What services do they have?	Is the spend reasonable?

▲ market information table

About staff	Types of data for retrieval and analysis
Work rate	How many services or treatments have been completed?
Popularity	How many clients are allotted to each stylist?
Work type	What numbers of different services have been provided?
Pay bonuses	Are there special incentives for staff to achieve?

efficiency and profitability

The average billing is a wonderful rule of thumb to show how productive your salon is. By taking the sales figure per month and dividing this by the number of clients in that time, you will arrive at the average bill. The cut and finish price is a useful guide. If the average bill works out around this figure or below, it will be hard for your salon to make a profit over a period of time. Where average billing is significantly higher than your cut and finish, this indicates strong additional services or retail sales.

How many clients does the business need to be efficient? You may think this is a strange question, since you know how many clients the business needs to be profitable.

The business break-even point is crucial for monitoring the current financial position. This tells you when the operation is profitable and, conversely, when you are falling behind. This measure will also help you to make some longer-term decisions, such as when

cut-backs are needed! As a manager you already have a target figure in mind. You know fairly accurately on a week-by-week basis what your break-even point is. Or do you?

The problem with targets is accurately setting them; they are vulnerable and always subject to fluctuations. This could be caused by a variety of accounting factors, such as the rent becoming due, the need to pay for stock, bank charges, interest payments etc.

Emergency situations must be considered, and these can rapidly blow a hole in the cash flow forecasts: the hot water immersion tank bursts! a stylist leaves at short notice! the salon is broken into!

There are also seasonal fluctuations and effects to be taken into account, such as summer shortage of staff cover, school holidays, family holidays, water shortages and so on, and the effects of winter, such as poor weather, treacherous road conditions, leaves on railway lines etc. Whatever the time of year, there will be some 'knock on' effect to your business.

projection and speculation

We can already accept that a salon's profitability is directly linked to the salon's overheads. A salon whose cost of sales is high will need to generate more income than a salon whose costs are low. What we should be doing is looking at the gross salon product, i.e. the total output from the salon, and in relation to this how well each of the individual stylists is doing within the team framework.

We can normally expect our regular clients to visit the salon on a 6-weekly basis. In addition to these will be the occasional clients who come less often. Although both the regular and occasional clients are important to the business, it is the regular clients that we can quantify within projections. The occasional clients are just subjects of speculation. The difference is between fact and fiction.

occupancy levels

In the Hotel and Catering sector there is a specific measurement for identifying when targets are being met. Rather than fixing figures on a weekly or monthly basis, companies will take a more general approach throughout their financial year. In addition to the detailed plans and cash flow forecasts that these companies have, they will also use their levels of occupancy as a 'yardstick'. This occupancy is an expected volume of trade measured as a percentage. In other words, they expect from the outset to achieve a minimum level of room occupancy throughout the year. This figure will vary according to whether the company is a large multinational combine such as Granada, Holiday Inns and the Hilton group, or a medium-sized operation such as Stakis Hotels or Travel Lodge. But even the small independents work on the same principle. Hotels, depending on their overheads, look for a minimum occupancy of 65–70 per cent.

Salons can take this approach too. If you take the business as a whole, you would expect all the members of the styling team to pull their weight. This level of contribution should be built into the business plan as an expectation or a performance indicator.

We need our stylists to be working near to their optimum potential, which means that they will be busy for most of the time during the working week. If we take a full-time stylist on a five-day-week, let's say that the average number of available appointments for each full working day is approximately 12. If we multiply this average of 12 by the number of working days, say 5, we arrive at 60. So this is the optimum number of available appointments within a week.

Now, if we again consider that regular clients return, on average, every six weeks, there will be 360 available appointments, i.e. $60 \times 6 = 360$. This leads us to believe that a stylist with roughly this number of regular clients on the database would be working flat out at 100 per cent occupancy.

Working to this rate is unusual and, although very time-efficient and cost-effective, would, in the long-term lead to other problems. Not having any facility for time flexibility will, in time, prove very stressful for the stylist and might:

- erode the standard of service quality being delivered to the client
- increase levels of tiredness for the operator
- allow insufficient time to provide other alternative services and treatments
- develop a work routine that is tedious and repetitive, and
- eventually lose clients!

We can now work back with these figures and look at the average occupancy for two different stylists. For example, a stylist has 280 clients over a six-weekly period; their occupancy is $280/360 \times 100 = 78$ per cent. Conversely, a stylist who has 320 clients over a six-weekly period has an occupancy of $320/360 \times 100 = 89$ per cent. As you can see, the maths is very simple.

Because the nature of the business is cyclical, i.e. we expect our regular clients to repeat their visit within a set time-frame, it is sometimes better to use this time-interval as the denominator in the calculation.

If we just looked at the financial returns as either weekly or monthly inputs, we would not be seeing specific trends – the business upturns or downturns

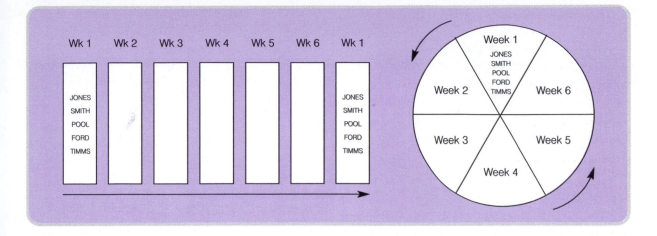

as they occur. Confusing? If we expect a stylist to service their regular clients over a six-weekly pattern, then we know when specific clients should be back.

As you can see in the figure, in week 1 we have clients Jones, Smith, Pool, Ford and Timms. Let's say that each client pays £50.00, so therefore Week 1 has generated £250.00. If we maintain this average throughout the six weeks, we generate £1,500.00. Mrs Jones contributes £50.00 × 8.666 (52 weeks divided by 6) = £433.00 per year to the business. Looking at the business over the year, we can expect £1,500.00 × 8.666 = £13,000.

Over the year without Mrs Jones we only achieve £1,450 × 8.666 = £12,565. This illustration shows that we are almost £500.00 down. Without the immediate recognition that a client has lapsed, the long-term impact is considerable.

Conversely, if Mrs Jones remains a regular client but her repeat cycle changes to 7 weeks because the stylist is too busy to fit her in, we arrive at £50.00 × 7.43 = £371.00, a loss of £61.00. Imagine if this scenario happened with all the customers; it could in effect wipe out all your profits!

One of the ways to combat situations like this would be always to prompt clients to book their next appointment before they leave the salon. You will then maintain good business, give good service and spot any anomalies as they occur, giving you the opportunity to remedy any potential problems promptly.

Computill Ltd

3

beginning to manage the business

■ records, systems and procedures

This part of the book aims to give you the necessary background information for beginning to manage the business. No business can be run properly without records, systems and procedures; this part will provide you with the basic essentials to achieve this.

Whether you are computer minded or not, you will find various tips and ideas here, together with plenty of simple illustrations to help you along the way.

■ routine duties

The day-to-day duties for the salon manager will involve the following activities:

- monitoring salon transactions
- allocating work
- maintaining the provision of stock
- managing client information.

We keep 'on top' of these duties by putting into place a variety of systems and procedures. These will help to ensure a standardised approach, quality assurance and good customer care. Looking at this in another way, let's think about hairdressing systems that we already take for granted. Can you imagine running a business without a till? Or booking in regular clients who have their hair coloured without having the correct tint in stock? Imagine the problems that would occur in a salon that never uses an appointment system! These thoughts may be ridiculous but they show the principle that we automatically take for granted certain essential business systems as cash registers (tills), stock control and appointments.

The level of sophistication within the business systems that you use within your salon will depend on the:

- abilities of your staff
- types of systems introduced
- time made available to maintain the systems
- financial resources available.

As hairdressers, your staff's abilities will be predominantly associated with delivering services and treatments to clients. It is therefore most likely that your staff will have a wide range of technical skills and little time to do anything else. Whereas your duties (which may include these skills) will also involve managing and making decisions about finance, people, market information and legislation.

One could argue that this skills' gap could provide the basis for specific training and development, but this is often not possible within a small business. You therefore need to focus on your particular business needs. What are the skills that are essential to the success of the business? What others are merely desirable? By analysing your business in this way you are:

- identifying possible training needs for employees
- prioritising the business functions
- starting to set minimum standards and requirements
- providing possible options for future directions.

You will need to develop a variety of systems and procedures that can easily be used by others.

The types of systems that you introduce will have cost implications for the business. Paper systems may be relatively inexpensive to produce but will involve a lot of time in planning, design and evaluation. On the other hand, the introduction of information technology to the business may be an expensive option but will provide many other longer-term benefits.

Regardless of which direction the business takes, i.e. the use of manual or automated systems, both options will need time devoted to the task of collecting and recording accurate information. Initially, this could mean that time will be required to be spent in training staff designated to use the systems. Then, on a daily basis, time should be allowed for the systems to be maintained and updated.

For further information on computers, see pages 50–53.

monitoring the daily transactions and events

This process will depend on the levels of automation and the systems that your business uses, i.e. whether you prefer:

- computer-based packages, or
- manual processing.

If you have a computer, it will operate using one of two types of software.

1. 'tailor made' bespoke software

Tailor made software is industry specific and consists of an integrated software package that records and manages all the transactions whilst the bills are being processed. This allows, during billing, automatic adjustments and updating to be made to client files, stock movements, services, treatments and stylist sales. Systems such as these provide useful reports that give comprehensive management information and save valuable time. The only drawback with these 'off the shelf' software packages is that report generation is built in and therefore you are limited to manipulating only the data that the software package is designed to provide. These systems tend to be expensive, so make sure that the features and benefits of the software meet your requirements. Finding an 'off the shelf' software package that meets your exact needs would be highly unlikely.

2. generally available software

Alternatively, you may use a partly automated system whereby data is supplied to the computer at other times than the 'point of sale'. This involves making entries to databases, spreadsheets, word processors and possibly an accounts package. The most commonly available software for this purpose is 'Microsoft Office' or 'Lotus Smartsuite'. Both of these packages are more than adequate in providing most business needs, although it is worth remembering that good working knowledge is essential and therefore specialist training will be necessary.

For further information on computers, see pages 50–53.

If you do not have access to computers, it is vitally important that your manual paper systems and records are adequately maintained. These will vary from salon to salon but here is a list of essentials:

- The appointment schedule
- Stock management and control
- Client records
- Daily/weekly financial summaries
- Staff records (performance and training)
- Monthly accounts records
- Methods for tracking and filing receipts, invoices etc.

the appointment schedule

At the centre of the business is the appointment recording system. In its simplest form, this tabular system will show, at a glance, the availability of appointments on either a daily, weekly or monthly basis. From this information the expected work load for each stylist can be deduced. The majority of salons will purchase a standard appointment book which contains columns with timed entries ready for completion.

This system is the core of the business and has the potential for providing a lot of other valuable information. Many salons find that they can integrate a number of other aspects of the salon into the recording system at no great expense, by developing their own systems and by pre-printing daily sheets according to their needs. From an organisational point of view there are many benefits in using and operating your own 'in-house appointment system' rather than using a standard book (see the figure on page 42).

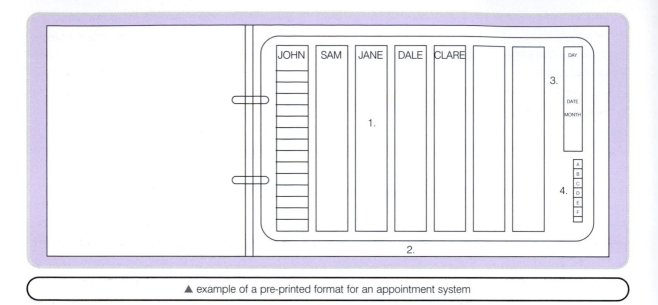

▲ example of a pre-printed format for an appointment system

In the example shown above, this 'tailor made' system incorporates a number of organisational and spatial differences that have clear advantages over 'bought' standard appointment books. In this example we see:

1. Columns which can be set for the number of stylists employed so that no wasted columns appear. There are suitable times of appointments which are linked to individual rates of work

2. Pages for recording appointments are on right-hand facing pages only, facilitating easier navigation throughout the calendar

3. Day, date and month are recorded at the top right-hand corner for easy access to future dates

4. A simple system can be incorporated for advancing from this day to any number of weeks in the future (see figure below).

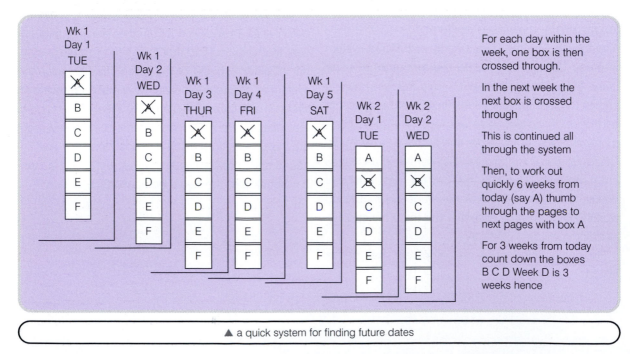

▲ a quick system for finding future dates

In the example in the figure at the bottom of page 42, six boxes marked A to F vertically from top to bottom are repeated across the page. Each complete working week is crossed through in pencil, the first week being A, the second week B and so on. In order to navigate quickly to 6 weeks into the future, just thumb through to the next weeks which have the 'cross' mark in box A. If you want to go 4 weeks into the future, just count down the boxes B,C,D,E, 1,2,3,4, and you are at week E which is 4 weeks away.

This is a simple but very accurate way of navigating through the calendar to make future appointments for your clients quickly and accurately. By setting an appointment page only on a right-hand facing page, you can then utilise the back of the page, overleaf, for other essential information. On this reverse side of each day page you can also pre-print all the daily summaries that you need. This could include areas for financial information, space for monitoring new customers and their addresses for updating information at a later time. See the example shown in the figure below.

The information contained on each day sheet can be transferred to your record systems at a later time.

computerised appointment systems

Computer-based appointment systems tend to fall into two types:

- mouse or keyboard actuated
- touch screen technology.

Both of these types of technology run similar software and in many cases look the same, the only difference being the input device. The input device is the method by which the software is operated. All contemporary software runs under Windows (™ Microsoft) or software that simulates the Windows environment, i.e. WIMP systems (*W*indows, *I*cons, *M*enus and *P*ointer)

The computerised appointment scheduler appears as a tabular view of the day's activities. Navigation through the calendar to future dates can be made by simple selection of objects linking the information.

Mouse or keyboard operation is by far the more popular of the two. It is widely used, less expensive

	SALES	BD	CBD	HL	PW	COL	DC		NEW	CONTACT BY
JOHN	125.00	3	3	1		1	1		1	advert in echo
SAM	156.00	4	2		2					
JANE	120.00	1	4	1		1			1	referral
DALE	D/OFF									
CLARE	HOL									
TOTAL	401.00	8	9	2	2	2	1			

Float	40	00
20s	60	00
10s	40	00
5s	5	00
Change	2	00
Cheque	120	00
Cards	174	00
Tot A	441	00

Till Outs	
Float	40.00
Petty Cash	0.00
Cash	401.00

New Customers	
John	Mrs Jenny Cark 01212 445676 1 Bolsover Court, Speedwell Bristol B3 2EW
Jane	Gail Timmings 0123 765431 Fl 2, Ford House, James Street Clarkside GL50 2DQ

▲ reverse side of appointment page

and compatible with all generally available computer packages. Selections of objects is made via the pointing device, i.e. the mouse, and text is applied using the standard keyboard.

Touch screens were initially popular in salons, when the use of computers was a new innovation. These are operated by simply touching the appropriate selection on screen. This technology is user friendly and expensive, but now unnecessary as most people in salons are computer literate.

stock management and control

Stock is a valuable asset belonging to the business, and it is essential that you monitor the movements of material resources on a daily basis. This includes both the sales of products to clients for use at home, as well as products used within the salon in order to provide services. Without effective control over the stock you may find that you have run out!

The effectiveness of monitoring stock will depend on the systems you operate:

■ computer-based systems, or
■ manual, paper-based systems

Computer-based systems are quickly becoming the preferred option for accurate stock management and it is expected that all small businesses will be utilising information technology (IT) by the year 2005. The computer can easily track stock movements, record sales and reorder, as well as providing up-to-date in-stock values.

As previously mentioned within this Part, there are two ways of using information technology within the salon. You may have a computer situated at reception, which runs a fully automated, integrated package at the point of sale: this method will automatically make stock adjustments as transactions are made. Or you may have a partially automated system, which involves the use of spreadsheet software, which will need updating at some other time within the salon office. Both methods are effective but have different advantages.

A computer system which is operated at the reception desk is best illustrated by the three diagrams shown below and on page 45.

Integrated computer software
In the first figure, an example of a computerised till receipt is shown on the left-hand side and the block on the right depicts the areas of information contained

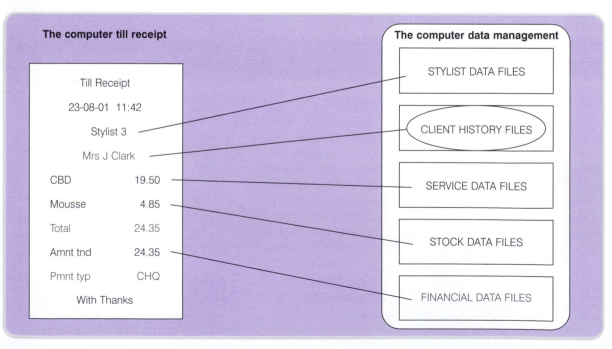

The computer till receipt

Till Receipt

23-08-01 11:42

Stylist 3

Mrs J Clark

CBD	19.50
Mousse	4.85
Total	24.35
Amnt tnd	24.35
Pmnt typ	CHQ

With Thanks

The Client History File

Came   Jeremy   Mr.

Carey   Jane   Miss

Channing   Samantha   Miss

Clark   Jenny   Mrs

Sales History:

23.08.01   11.42   24.35 CHQ

Services   CBD
Products   Mousse

Stylist   3

within the computer. As the client pays her bill, information is recorded relating to Staff, Clients, Services, Stock and Financial summaries.

In the second figure, the client history file, we see that each client has an individual record within a database that resembles a card file index system. As the

bill is processed, the computer sends the relevant information to each of these card files and updates the information on them automatically.

In the third figure, the stock data file, we see that within each card file, data is held for a different family of products.

The Stock Data File

The computer makes automatic adjustments in respect to:

Amounts
Sales
Minimum holding levels
Sizes
Types

Hairspray

Shampoo

Mousse

#1 L'Oreal Tech Ni Art
Type: Volumising Root Lift Mousse 150ml
In stock   11   Sold this week   4
Flag auto re-order when in stock = 5

 # 2
Type: Protective Mousse Firm Hold 150ml
In stock   11   Sold this week   4
Flag auto re-order when in stock = 5

The text shown in bold on the card file has fixed fields and provides identification details for the products, whereas the non-bold text contains numerical information in variable fields and is automatically adjusted when sales are activated through till procedures.

This type of program is specifically designed software, which links together several card files by passing shared information within specific fields; this is called a relational database.

We discussed earlier in this Part the possibility of running a partially automated system, utilising commonly available (off the shelf) software. If you are familiar with these integrated suites for office management you can easily set up your own Stock Management Database.

Manual, paper-based systems will be the alternative option for the small businesses that are not yet IT aware. Unfortunately, these systems do not provide the flexibility and power of computers or the extent of their management information, but should be adequate and reliable in salons that have smaller stock-holding levels. This is assuming, of course, that those involved monitor stock levels accurately.

The example shown provides a format for a paper-based stock recording system. We can see that in the first column there is a range of product types, i.e. L'Oreal Kerastase. Each family of products – shampoos, conditioners etc. – can be grouped together. In the next column we have identified the product size.

The next two columns are each repeated three times; these contain space to enter the date, product minimum holding levels, amounts in stock and quantities for order. Orders are placed when amounts in stock fall beneath the minimum holding levels.

By repeating the columns, stock movements can be monitored over several stock counts. This can easily identify trends and patterns of faster and slower moving lines.

Stock Master		Date	12/Sept 00		Date			Date		
L'Oreal Retail Products	Size	Minimum Holding Level	In Stock	Order	Minimum Holding Level	In Stock	Order	Minimum Holding Level	In Stock	Order
KERASTASE										
Neutrative Hair Baths										
Satin	250ml	4	③	1 box						
Enriching	250ml	4	4	0						
Revitalising	250ml	3	7	0						
Neutrative Treatments										
Protein cond	250ml	4	②	1 box						
Elixir Vital	250ml	4	②	1 box						
Masqu. Thick	400ml	2	4	0						
Masqu. Fine	400ml	2	4	0						

▲ manual stock recording system

products

product branding

Your product manufacturers have one objective, that is, to sell you as much product as they can.

We are now entering a new commercial age, the age of corporate globalisation. Large multinational companies with diverse activities find it more cost-effective to acquire their desired brands and markets sectors by purchasing their smaller competitors. The household 'branded' names continue to exist even when company parent lineage changes dramatically. These types of moves will eventually lead to less choice, higher pricing and more control by the manu-facturers. Branding in the '90s has already had a great impact upon marketing. However, it seems that this trend is set to continue way into the next century. This has been made evident by the success of companies such as Virgin, whose involvements are wide ranging, from travel to financial services, music to cola.

The idea when a brand name is created (or bought) is that extensive marketing, promotions, research and development will bring about public awareness of the product. Once the image and market are defined, the target audience will buy that commodity.

Defining your pitch within the marketplace is always very difficult. It relies upon several issues, namely 'the marketing mix' or the 4 P's (see page 32). You should be aware of the importance of creating your own brand image. This all-important public image will be based upon the expertise of your staff, your trading position, the look of your salon, the variety of services you provide and the products that you choose to provide.

Stock control is really about monitoring product quantity, quality and security whilst managing supply and demand. As manager, the maintenance of prod-uct quality and security is vitally important and more often delegated to members of your staff; whereas the decisions regarding supply and demand are definitely your domain. Arriving at the right balance for cost-effective supply to meet demand can be very difficult.

retailing

The fierce competition in hairdressing, together with the rise of professional home-hair-care products has led to a retailing boom. At the forefront of this are inno-vative stylists and salons that have realised the poten-tial of the in-salon 'one stop shop'.

In the future, even more clients will be seeking the professional advice that only their hairdressers can provide about the products that they should be using. Sales of all product categories, except home perms, are rising year on year – sprays and colourants by 12 per cent each, shampoos by 15 per cent and condi-tioners by a massive 18 per cent.

With the total market expanding by about 7 per cent annually, there's still ample scope for further profitable development at all market levels: from the prescriptive ranges of Kerastase by L'Oreal and System Professional by Wella at the upper market end, right through to 'cheap and cheerful' products at the lower end.

what is retailing?

Retailing is selling to consumers, in either single or bulk quantities, over the counter, off the shelf, on doorsteps and by mail order. If it is done well, retailing will enhance the image of both the salon and sales-person by adding professionalism and value to the

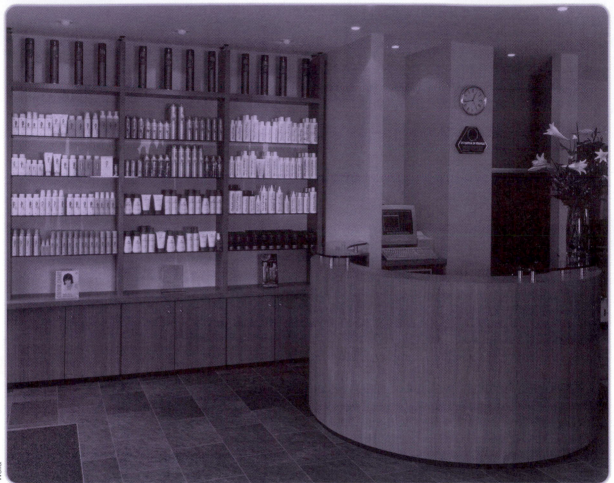

Wella

total service. In-salon shopping meets clients' needs, fulfils their desires and makes them feel good. What more could they want?

The key elements to good selling are:

- listening to the clients and hearing what they say, asking questions and showing interest
- addressing the client by name
- showing empathy (putting yourself in the client's place) and establishing a rapport
- recognising non-verbal body language (dilated pupils, 'I approve'; ear-rubbing, 'I've heard enough')
- identifying needs and helping clients to reach buying decisions
- knowing your products and services

- summarising the features, or user benefits
- thinking positively, and projecting confidence and enthusiasm.

The indicators of bad selling are:

- doing all the talking
- not listening – not 'hearing'
- interrupting – but never letting the clients interrupt you, therefore losing the opportunity to provide extra information
- hard sell
- hollow threats – 'You won't get it cheaper anywhere else'
- knocking the opposition
- knowing nothing about the product
- blinding clients with science
- insisting the client should buy the product.

The 'bad' list is longer because bad selling still continues. The effect of little or no training at all can be reinforced by the fact that most salons will claim that 80 per cent of their business comes from 20 per cent of their salesforce.

creating the right selling atmosphere

'Closing' a sale is not a final plea that occurs in the dying moments of a pitch for business. It is the whole process, from that moment when a client walks in: the warm, friendly welcome, relaxing ambience, focused attention, pleasant and friendly manner, talking his/her language, heeding their inner concerns, quietly suggesting appropriate solutions ('We should be able to help you'; 'Have you thought about...?').

Retail professionals call it 'creating the right selling atmosphere' – one that stimulates people to buy. You must remember It is people you're dealing with, not robots! Therefore, simply selling on technicalities doesn't motivate clients. People don't buy formulas – they buy a result.

merchandising

Manufacturers would have us believe that there is a new approach to salon retailing and the buzzword is 'merchandising'. There are distinct advantages and disadvantages to the merchandising approach. Hairdressing product manufacturers have now copied the tried-and-tested methods of successful retailers. This can be explained in the following way.

In supermarkets, products have a set pattern in which they are laid out. Within this pattern other patterns occur. When we use a particular supermarket, we get used to the layout, i.e. we know that as we enter, we first see the newsagent's kiosk selling papers, magazines, tobacco and confectionery. Moving on through the store we will find the fresh produce market stalls. Somewhere close at hand are the delicatessen, the bakery, the fishmongers and the meats. In-between will be tinned foods, dairy produce and so on. These are laid out in a specific style. On each of the product shelves, families of products appear. These products are positioned edge to edge and several items deep.

'pile it high and wide'

Hairdressing manufacturers would like salons to adopt this approach and in principle the concept is fine: a clearly defined area with attractive, well-lit, product lines and comprehensive ranges including shampoos, conditioners, treatments and styling.

Products placed edge to edge in colour-coordinated groupings on purpose-built shelving encourage clients to 'shop' when they visit your salon. This in essence is good business.

Elsewhere within the salon the 'message' can be reinforced by creating attractive displays. This will encourage clients to talk about products and ask for advice.

This approach to salon merchandising provides a professional image, but it can be very expensive. Product merchandising in this way is sold in measured units. Each metre of product shelving will be filled edge to edge, several products deep. This eliminates the need for additional storage since the shelves become your store room. Merchandising is fine provided that you have a good turnover of stock. Limit the numbers of stock purchases for product lines that are slow moving. Stock that does not sell will gather dust, be superseded by newer lines and will leave you with high 'in hand' values at the end of your financial year, which may well affect your profits.

merchandising 'nitty gritty'

Behind the scenes, market research is used to find out clients' likes or dislikes. Along with this data, suppliers ensure that we get the right packaging and promotional support materials so that products can be displayed to their mutually beneficial, full potential.

Product presentation is assisted by:

- point-of-sale merchandising, open cabinet display, shelf displays
- shelftalkers – printed promotional slips/cards fixed to or dangling from shelves; 'mobile' ones that bob or bounce deliver best results
- eye-catching displays that are instantly informative; locate them where they'll be seen – at reception, or centrally in treatment areas

- arrangement of popular lines at eye level, with price details; use 'price watch' stickers
- linking displays with money-off and other special offers – first-visit, loyalty, recommend-a-friend discounts, and other promotional tie-ins.

good 'deals'

One other buying practice that you should be very clear about is buying stock at heavily discounted prices. This will usually mean that you have to buy well in advance of the business's needs. In principle this activity makes good sense, because it is logical to obtain the best price possible.

Bear in mind the wider issues of bulk purchasing. The stock will need to be insured and will take up additional storage space. More importantly (and to be borne in mind elsewhere in this book) is the fact that a large invoice will arrive and might coincide with other planned payments. This may have devastating affects on the cash flow forecast!

There is still a lot to be said for minimising stock and only purchasing sufficient materials that may be required on a week-to-week basis.

■ client record management

If there is one aspect of the modern salon that necessitates the power of the PC it is client record management.

Your clients' service records are a physical history, whereas your client record management is the future.

Without up-to-date accurate records you have no control over your business. Accurate client records will enable you to:

- contact your clients
- monitor client visits
- plan your expected pattern of repeat business
- monitor patterns of services, treatments and buying habits
- plan promotions and special offers
- gain market information
- identify market opportunities.

Not all of these topics will be of interest to everyone, because different salons operate in different ways. Some of these issues are reactive and others proactive. The reactive issues respond to the information that is recorded under client history, i.e. services, treatments, personal information. Whereas proactive issues provide business opportunities for the future, especially for marketing purposes.

It would be extremely difficult to manage information that was to be used proactively without the use of computerised client databases. With only paper-based systems, how long would it take you to find the information in this market analysis scenario?

> Taking the total number of clients that your salon has, how many of the student clients have had highlights in the past six months? From these, how many have not yet revisited the salon?

A paper-based card file system may be able to provide the necessary information but will be difficult to sort under the specified criteria within reasonable time-scales.

computerised client databases

The power of the PC provides the small business with amazing marketing opportunities. By using a modern database software package, difficult operations and procedures can be mastered in a relatively short time.

In the figures that follow we see an example form used within a database and a table that defines some of the technical jargon.

In the example form shown on page 51 we can see a variety of fields for which data is entered, referred to as a Field label: CL.LAST refers to the field client's last name, CL.FIRST to the client's first name etc. There are also check boxes referring to months of the year and radio buttons relating to service type and age range.

HEAD LINE CLIENT INFORMATION

CL. LAST   CL. FIRST   CL. TITLE   STYLIST

CL. ADD1   CL. ADD2   CL. ADD3

CL. PCODE   CL. TEL

SERV. HIST

CBD HL COL WC

J	0 0 0 0 0	
F	0 0 0 0 0	O -14
M	0 0 0 0 0	O 15-21
A	0 0 0 0 0	O 22-35
M	0 0 0 0 0	O 36-49
J	0 0 0 0 0	O 50+
J	0 0 0 0 0	
A	0 0 0 0 0	
S	0 0 0 0 0	
O	0 0 0 0 0	

▲ database form on screen

typical database terms

Field	The smallest piece of a database into which single pieces of information are typed within the area
Field types	Fields may contain the following: text, numeric, date, time, memo information
Record	A record contains a group of related fields
Field label	A name given to a field that enables the person entering the data to recognise the type of information required
Forms	An arrangement of fields in an easy-to-view format
Worksheet	A table of information similar to a spreadsheet
Search	A way of locating information that matches specific criteria
Sort	A way of organising database records in a specific order
Report	A way of extracting printed management information that matches specific criteria
Mail merge	A system for linking wordprocessed documents to personnel data held within a database and for printing this information out

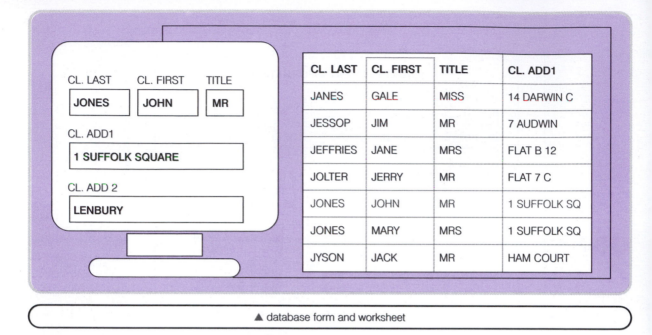

CL. LAST	CL. FIRST	TITLE	CL. ADD1
JANES	GALE	MISS	14 DARWIN C
JESSOP	JIM	MR	7 AUDWIN
JEFFRIES	JANE	MRS	FLAT B 12
JOLTER	JERRY	MR	FLAT 7 C
JONES	JOHN	MR	1 SUFFOLK SQ
JONES	MARY	MRS	1 SUFFOLK SQ
JYSON	JACK	MR	HAM COURT

CL. LAST — JONES
CL. FIRST — JOHN
TITLE — MR
CL. ADD1 — 1 SUFFOLK SQUARE
CL. ADD 2 — LENBURY

▲ database form and worksheet

In the example above we can choose the view that we want to see:

1. the form which holds a single client's record on screen, *or*
2. the tabular worksheet which contains all the records within the database.

what do databases do?

A database manages, handles and transfers information. Modern packages have a similar look and feel although their operational procedures may be very different. With modern software you would be working with 'commonly accepted' business systems, i.e. using forms, generating reports, writing letters and mailing labels.

Most database software will feature the following facilities:

✓ Pre-designed databases and templates for customer service, employee management, stock management and invoicing
✓ Built-in forms for simple completion with the flexibility of free form design
✓ Comprehensive report generators
✓ Mail merge facilities with support for label printing
✓ Extensive sort and data-retrieval capabilities.

At the point where all the salons clients are added to the computer, the real power of the database becomes apparent.

Access to the files can be sorted and retrieved in several ways. A search condition is created, usually by requesting the computer to FIND. At this point the user is confronted with a blank form as in the example shown on page 53. Here a character string is entered within one or more fields and perhaps a search condition is applied so that exact data can be found.

We see that the search criteria used, JONES in field CL.LAST and SAM in field STYLIST, have found two records. If only JONES had been typed in, four records would have matched.

Conversely, if we wanted an exact search for Sam's client Mr Jones, we would have entered MR into the TITLE field.

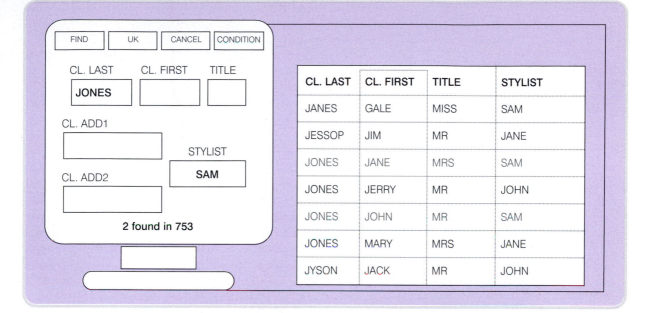

part 4

beginning to manage
money

4

beginning to manage money

■ summary

In order to manage your business effectively, you will need to set up records and systems that will track all the financial transactions. These accounting systems will show the income to the business during the month, the VAT considerations and be able to accurately track all the expenditure.

Monthly accounting can be made simpler if you have tight controls over the everyday till transactions, the daily and weekly summaries as well as any other financial activities. This can only be achieved by keeping accurate records, and for a small business you will at least need:

Cash book – which will (1) record sales and payments, (2) record payments in and out of the bank and (3) show VAT on qualifying payments
Wages book – a separate system for recording salaries and any deductions made (taxes, NICs)
VAT records – showing how VAT has been calculated
Petty cash book – covering small cash expenses and identifying any VAT.

Without a proper set of business records, you would not know what your financial position is at any particular moment. You need to know at any time:

■ How much you owe to your suppliers
■ How much money you have in the bank.

■ money in general

The diagram below illustrates the movements of funds into and out of the business.

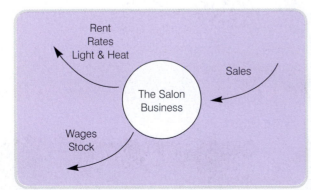

As you can see from the diagram, money comes into the business generated by sales from services and treatments, i.e. income; whilst costs, both fixed and variable, go out of the business, i.e. expenditure.

income

Income to the business will enter the till in different ways. Money entering the till in the form of cash will provide immediate funds, whereas other forms of transactions such as cheques and cards may take several days to process.

Cheques received at the till would normally be paid into the business bank account at some later date. At the time when these cheques are presented to the bank, it could take up to a further 5 working days for the bank to credit the business account. When your business is working to a tight budget this delay must be considered, especially when standing orders or direct payments are scheduled to go out.

Card payments are more often made via electronic terminals as opposed to manual imprinters. These funds are paid directly into the business account by BACS (Banking Automated Clearing Systems). The contract that you have with the card processing company will state whether these funds are to be credited into the account on either a daily or a weekly basis. However, it is worth remembering that service charges for daily credits to the business account will be more expensive than one deposit weekly.

expenditure

Money going out of the business account to cover expenses may be debited in a number of different ways.

Business cheques will be drafted to pay for incoming invoices, for items such as goods, advertising and telephone, whereas standing orders and direct debits may be set up to cover other costs such as rent, rates, electricity and gas. Other withdrawals on the trading account may be set up in the form of transfers to other accounts to cover, for example, proprietor's drawings, staff wages, loans and overdrafts.

The business's expenditure can be looked at in two different ways:

fixed costs

Fixed costs are those costs that are not affected by the levels of business carried out. So, regardless of how much, or of how little income is generated, these costs will remain the same, i.e. the rent for the premises, the business rates and your commercial insurances will still have to be paid.

When you devise a cash flow forecast, these costs are known from the outset and can be budgeted for on a regular basis (see figure on page 76).

variable costs

Variable costs will be directly proportional to the levels of business, i.e. as sales increase, costs will rise accordingly. For example, as the stylists generate more income for the salon, their salaries will increase with additional commissions. When more services are being provided, extra stock will be used.

When devising a cash flow forecast for these costs it will be more difficult to calculate the figures.

■ payment methods: advantages and disadvantages

cash

✓ Provides immediate funds for the business
✓ Still a popular option with clients for smaller billings
✓ Has no hidden transaction or banking charges

✗ Can create problems for business security

cheque

✓ Has no hidden transaction or banking charges

✗ Rapidly being superseded by debit cards
✗ Slow 'pipeline' for providing cleared funds
✗ Does not always guarantee payment even with cheque guarantee card

✗ Create extra administration for paying procedures

debit card

✓ Ideal for quick, efficient processing
✓ Provides immediate authorisation and hence 'good funds' to be deposited into the account
✓ Provides a simpler alternative to cheques

✗ Will incur a flat rate charge to the 'merchant' for the benefit of operation
✗ Can easily be used fraudulently, so extra care for security must be maintained

credit card

✓ Ideal for quick, efficient processing
✓ Provides immediate authorisation and hence 'good funds' to be deposited into the account
✓ Provides useful alternatives to 'I would like to have my hair done, but I haven't got any money at the moment'

✗ Will incur a percentage of billing charge to the 'merchant' for the benefit of operation
✗ Can easily be used fraudulently, so extra care for security must be maintained

charge card

✓ Ideal for quick, efficient processing
✓ Provides immediate authorisation and hence 'good funds' to be deposited into the account
✓ Provides useful alternatives to 'I would like to have my hair done, but I haven't got any money at the moment'

✗ Will incur a percentage of billing charge to the 'merchant' for the benefit of operation
✗ Can easily be used fraudulently, so extra care for security must be maintained

■ till operations
basics

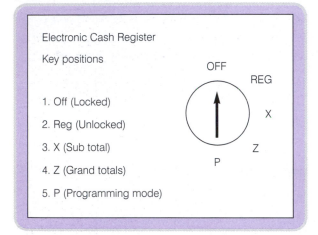

Electronic Cash Register

Key positions

OFF
REG

1. Off (Locked)
2. Reg (Unlocked)

X

3. X (Sub total)
4. Z (Grand totals)

Z

P

5. P (Programming mode)

Electronic Cash Registers are becoming increasingly more sophisticated. The basic functions are shown in the diagram above. Here we see the five basic turnkey positions:

Till off This manually prevents the till from being opened or operated.

Till in register mode This illustrates the normal register mode used for transactions.

X position This allows for sub totals to be generated and printed out without affecting the final grand total operations.

Z position This provides a final end summary, giving a complete transaction breakdown and grand total.

P position This will allow the user to access the programming mode, which is used to define or redefine the key pad functions and facilities.

On more advanced machines there are detailed printouts and summaries, pre-set keys that can be programmed to equate to set tariffs and useful management information.

electronic payment systems

Salons that have agreements with companies such as Barclays Merchant Services, American Express Sales and Establishments etc. can offer the facility for payment by card. The salon operating the payment system will, in return, pay a fee to the card operator for the benefit. Debit cards such as Solo and Delta are charged at a fixed rate, whereas credit and charge cards take a percentage of the billing amount. The amount charged to the merchant for handling credit and charge cards can be negotiated but will depend upon card turnover.

Payments made by debit, charge and credit card via electronic terminals, such as P.D.Q., are authorised during the transaction process; this provides the 'cleared funds' that will be deposited into the business current account either on a daily or weekly basis. (This process includes all transactions except those carried out under fraudulent circumstances; this would include card theft, tampered/damaged cards and mail order when customers are not present at the point of sale.)

The electronic terminal consists of a key pad and card swipe input with LED output recording each step of the transaction procedure. In addition to this, a carbonless two-ply receipt roll provides a customer till receipt. The unit is connected to the card companies via a modem through a telephone cable link.

the procedure

1. Check that the terminal display is in sale mode.
2. Confirm that a sale is to be made by pressing button **yes**.
3. The terminal will request **Swipe card**; do this, ensuring that the magnetic strip passes over the reader head and retain the card in your hand. (In some cases the magnetic strip cannot be read by the card swipe reader; in this situation, the complete card number must be keyed manually into the terminal. This does not necessarily indicate that there is any need for suspicion, but inspect the card for any signs of tampering.)
4. Enter **Amount** using the key pad to input the total amount of purchases. (If you make a mistake, you can clear the figures using the **CLR** button.)
5. Press **Enter** to connect the terminal to the card company, first by **Dialling** and then by prompting the message **Connection Made**.

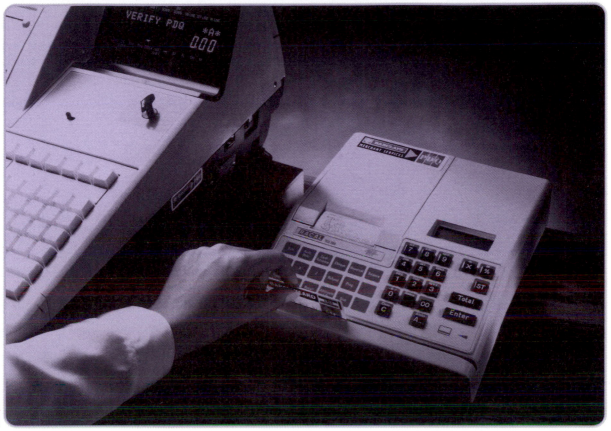

Sharp

6. Customer details are automatically accessed. After a few moments a message will authorise payment by showing **Auth code** for which a code number will be printed onto the receipt along with the other purchase details. Conversely, if the transaction is declined, 'card not accepted' will be displayed.

7. Whilst holding the card, tear off the two-part receipt and ask the cardholder to sign in ball-point pen in the space provided.

8. Check that the signature matches the signature on the card and return the top signed copy with the card to the customer.

seeking authorisation

If the total value of services and/or goods exceeds your pre-arranged floor limit, or if you are in any way suspicious of the card, its presenter or the circumstances of the sale, you must seek authorisation. Having ensured that all the items, in addition to services, are not within the customer's reach, take the card and the completed and signed sales voucher, with a ball-point pen to the telephone. Dial your card authorisation operator and be ready to provide the following information:

☑ The number that is embossed on the customer's card

☑ The salon's merchant number (a unique number registered with the card operating companies)

☑ The amount of the transaction.

Occasionally you may be asked to obtain some form of positive identification from the customer presenting the card.

When the sale is authorised you will be given a code that may include numbers and letters. You must write this code in the **Authorisation Code Box** on the sales voucher.

If the request is declined, no reason will be given. You should return the card to your customer and ask for some other form of payment.

code 10 authorisation calls

There are times when it is necessary to seek authorisation for a transaction but it is not possible to speak freely over the telephone – particularly if you are suspicious of the circumstances surrounding the transaction.

To avoid any difficulties when it is not possible to speak freely, you simply state that this is a **code 10 call**; the operator will then understand your predicament and will deal with your call sympathetically. If you are able to speak freely and are suspicious of the circumstances surrounding the transaction, let the authorisation operator know immediately.

In the following sections we look more closely at specific business financial controls. The first sections relate to the daily and weekly housekeeping, whereas later on we look at monthly accounting in the cash book, VAT records and financial planning.

daily financial summaries

The way in which you record your daily summaries is up to you, but be advised that, if you are considering keeping the end-of-day Till roll (Z reading) as your only

'hard copy', Inland Revenue will take a dim view. So be warned!

In Part 3, Beginning to Manage the Business, on pages 42 and 43 we provided an illustration of a simple form that can be pre-printed for the recording of daily activities. Whatever accounting methods you choose to devise, you must, at least, cover the following operations:

- Cash, cheque and card payments
- Payments from the till (with receipts)
- Balances and any discrepancies
- Gift vouchers or other similar non-cash payments
- Allowance for cash float.

monitoring till transactions

These days, everyone seems to be too busy: 'I haven't time for that'; 'I'll do that later'; 'I'll make a note and I'll call back later'. This probably seems familiar. Prioritising your time is essential (see the section on Time management at the end of Part 1, Planning for Business, pages 22 and 23). There are some activities that need close observance in order for the business to survive. Such aspects relate to financial control,

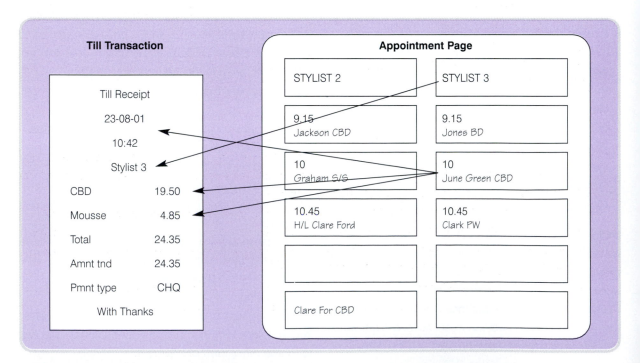

stock movement and service standards, which are essential to your business. Sometimes just sampling the till receipts will provide an indication of the strengths and weaknesses of these aspects.

In the example till receipt shown on page 60, we see that Stylist 3 has introduced a sale:

- From a service provision point of view, is the time-scale reasonable, i.e. is she working to time?
- Does the service relate to the appointment?
- Are there any retail sales to be accounted for?
- How was payment made?
- How will the client's visit be recorded?
- Are there any VAT implications?
- Are there any commissions that need to be recorded?

In the example on this page, we look at the end-of-day till roll.

From this example, we can see the breakdown by stylist, service and payment. All these aspects are important and should be recorded in your day-to-day systems.

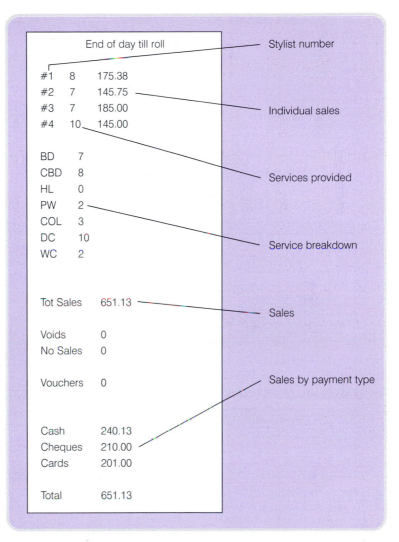

◼ weekly financial summaries
end-of-week records

At the end of each week you should compile a composite record of all the day-to-day activities for future reference. In the next two figures we illustrate the type and diversity of information that will need to be kept. The first illustration (page 62) covers the financial aspects day by day, whereas the second illustration (page 63) covers the service activities.

receipts, invoices and petty cash

Keeping track of all the business expenses is very important. These business purchases will probably fall into two kinds:

1. Relatively inexpensive purchases which are needed daily will be recorded as canteen items, things such as milk, coffee and tea; cleaning materials; other items such as stationery, magazines and pens.
2. Expensive purchases that arise through normal trading, such as stock and equipment.

Monday

	Sales	Retail
Sty 1		
Sty 2		
Sty 3		
Sty 4		
Cash		
Chqs		
Card		
Discreps		
TOTALS		

Tuesday

	Sales	Retail
Sty 1		
Sty 2		
Sty 3		
Sty 4		
Cash		
Chqs		
Card		
Discreps		
TOTALS		

Wednesday

	Sales	Retail
Sty 1		
Sty 2		
Sty 3		
Sty 4		
Cash		
Chqs		
Card		
Discreps		
TOTALS		

Thursday

	Sales	Retail
Sty 1		
Sty 2		
Sty 3		
Sty 4		
Cash		
Chqs		
Card		
Discreps		
TOTALS		

Friday

	Sales	Retail
Sty 1		
Sty 2		
Sty 3		
Sty 4		
Cash		
Chqs		
Card		
Discreps		
TOTALS		

Saturday

	Sales	Retail
Sty 1		
Sty 2		
Sty 3		
Sty 4		
Cash		
Chqs		
Card		
Discreps		
TOTALS		

Week totals

	Sales	Retail
Sty 1		
Sty 2		
Sty 3		
Sty 4		
Cash		
Chqs		
Card		
Discreps		
TOTALS		
VAT ON SALES		

WEEKLY FINANCIAL SUMMARY

Monday	Sty1	Sty2	Sty3	Sty4
CBD				
WC				
BD				
PW				
HL				
COL				
SS				
TOTALS				
NEW				

Tuesday	Sty1	Sty2	Sty3	Sty4
CBD				
WC				
BD				
PW				
HL				
COL				
SS				
TOTALS				
NEW				

Wednesday	Sty1	Sty2	Sty3	Sty4
CBD				
WC				
BD				
PW				
HL				
COL				
SS				
TOTALS				
NEW				

Thursday	Sty1	Sty2	Sty3	Sty4
CBD				
WC				
BD				
PW				
HL				
COL				
SS				
TOTALS				
NEW				

Friday	Sty1	Sty2	Sty3	Sty4
CBD				
WC				
BD				
PW				
HL				
COL				
SS				
TOTALS				
NEW				

Saturday	Sty1	Sty2	Sty3	Sty4
CBD				
WC				
BD				
PW				
HL				
COL				
SS				
TOTALS				
NEW				

Totals	Sty1	Sty2	Sty3	Sty4
CBD				
WC				
BD				
PW				
HL				
COL				
SS				
TOTALS				
NEW				

WEEKLY SERVICE SUMMARY

The difference between these two is the way in which they are accounted for. It is far easier to account for payments that you make by business cheque or card, than ones where you pay cash. However, in certain situations, this must be done.

Normally, when dealing with a product manufacturer or wholesale supplier, you can expect to be invoiced for the goods received. The supplier's terms will allow up to 30 days for payment. So, if you are ordering on a weekly basis, you may receive a number of deliveries throughout the month.

At the end of the month, you will receive a statement identifying all invoices for that accounting period and a request for payment is then made. This payment would normally be made by cheque. So from this procedure you can see that a lot a paper is generated:

1. You place an order with the supplier

2. They dispatch to you the goods along with a delivery note

3. Then the invoice is sent

4. At the end of the payment cycle, a statement arrives

5. You write and send off a cheque

6. This can be tracked on the bank statement when it arrives.

In the circumstances of petty cash payments you do not have this same ease of accountability or tracking. Don't get into the habit of taking money from the till as it is paid out and putting the receipts in. The easiest way to account for petty cash purchase is to set up a separate system (see figure below).

One way of doing this would be with a lockable tin and duplicate receipt book. Each week, a sum is removed from the trading account, for example £30.00. This would then be placed into a secure, lockable cash tin and an entry made into the duplicate book, which should state the amount deposited, and the date for the week ending. When purchases are made they are recorded in the book and their receipts are attached to the page. At the end of the week the totals are calculated and the money is balanced. This

£30.00 AT START OF WEEK

£26.89 WEEKS PURCHASES

£3.11 LEFT OVER

OF WHICH £1.10 IS VAT DEDUCTABLE

Petty Cash for Week Ending 10 Oct

Amount added £30.00

ITEM	COST	VAT
6/10 CORRECTION FLUID	0.99	0.15
7/10 TEA	2.50	—
7/10 COFFEE	4.25	—
8/10 MAGAZINES	10.00	—
9/10 WINDOW CLEAN	2.80	—
10/10 LIGHT BULBS	6.35	.95
TOTALS	26.89	1.10

is then repeated throughout the month until they are entered into the monthly cash book, see the figure on page 64.

monitoring the bank account

Entries to the business account book would normally be made on a monthly basis (see page 66). This will provide you with a month-by-month trading picture, but as we have already stated, careful notice should be taken regarding the income and expenditure upon the trading account.

Bank statements (unless specifically requested) will be posted to you on a monthly basis, or relevant to the number of transactions on the account. This state-ment will itemise in dated order the deposits made into the account and the withdrawals made from the account.

This snapshot of account history is important, par-ticularly when you need to reconcile the bank account. However, this statement may often arrive too late to make financial adjustments or even avoid unneces-sary and expensive overdrawn situations. It is vitally important that you keep a close check on the transac-tions that occur on a day-to-day basis. The following example shows how you can produce a simple form that can be completed daily, to account for move-ments within the business account.

Bank Account
Sheet number ... 17......   Dates from .. 1/3/00 .... to ....

Date	Transaction Type	Credit Debit	Item	Amount	balance
1/3 00	Night safe	+	Paid In	1,540.80	4,540
6/3	stand/ord	–	Midlands electricity	175	4,365
6/3	BACS	+	Barclays merchant services	942.56	5,307.56
6/3	Trans	–	Drawings	1,750	3,557.56
7/3	cheque	–	chq no. 610 (loreal)	1,245.90	2,311.66
8/3	night safe	+	Paid in	1,020.90	3,332.56
10/3	Direct debit	–	rates x county council	235.40	3,097.16
13/3	Trans to savs	–	rent	425	2,672.16
13/3	BACS	+	Barclays merchant services	1,034.56	3,706.72
15/3	cheque	–	chq. no. 611 (C. P. wages)	1,192	2,514.72
15/3	cheque	–	chq. no. 612 (F. G. wages)	645.50	1,869.22
15/3	cheque	–	chq. no. 613 (M. G. wages)	850	1,019.22

Notes	Standing Orders	Direct Debits	Transfers
Dates			
6th of month	MEB £175.00		Drawings 1,750.00
10th		Rates 235.40	
13th			Rent 425.00
27th		Insurs 57.00	

single-entry book-keeping
monthly accounts (cash book)

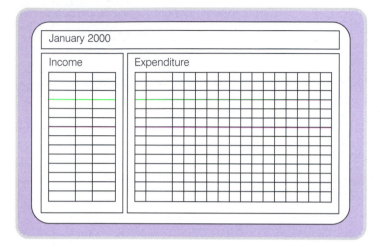

The cash book will contain the monthly record for all receipts and payments in connection with the business. Your accountant will advise on obtaining and setting up the correct type of accounts records. This may, depending on the size of your business, be simple or quite involved where large entities are concerned. The illustrations later in this text refer to analysed cash books. The advantage of this accounting system is that you can easily see at any point within the trading year how much you have spent on, say, advertising or training. (Analysis books vary in size and format, the main difference between them being the number of columns available for entries.) In the following diagrams you can see how the information is set out. Above we see that your receipts (income) are on the left and your payments (expenditure) are on the right.

The column headings on the income side of the page within the cash book should look like this:

Date	Gross (Receipts)	VAT	Net (Receipts)	Deposit/Banked

making entries into the cash book
income

For each day when sales are generated within the month, the gross, net, VAT and banked values are written into the book. The figure below shows entries for one week in January.

The column totals are completed to the end of the month and the values written in. The Deposit or Banked column should be reconciled against the bank statement to ensure that all the credits are correct.

Income January 2000

Date	Gross	VAT	Net	Banked
↓	↓			
continued from beginning of month				
Monday 10th	375.25	55.89	319.36	
Tuesday 11th	480.55	71.57	408.98	1,000.45
Wednesday 12th	512.25	76.29	435.96	
Thursday 13th	420.20	62.58	357.62	
Friday 14th	525.78	78.31	447.47	
Saturday 15th	725.25	108.02	617.23	1,245.67
continued throughout the month				
↓	↓			
Totals	3,039.28	452.66	2,586.62	2,246.12

expenditure

In the next illustration, showing the expenditure section, you can see that each of the columns is headed in relation to business expenses. The first entries relate to cheques that have been drawn. These entries are in date order and provide a cross-reference to the cheque number.

Each line relates to a payee showing, reading from left to right, the amount paid, the VAT, if applicable, and then the amount is rewritten within the appropriate column for accounts analysis. This is then completed for all the cheques drawn within the monthly accounting period.

Beneath the cheque payments are the direct payments/standing orders and finally any cash payments that have been made.

At the bottom of each column the totals can be completed. These can be cross-checked to verify the sums. The last column is a *Sundries* column to provide a general column that doesn't fit neatly into other areas. Regular payments, however, should have a column of their own; only items such as the purchase of new equipment or, say, a PAYE payment need to be entered into the sundries column.

If you have written cheques for specific items, say a replacement tumble drier, or have made payments for unusual sundry items such as flood-light bulbs, it might not always be clear what the payment was for. So when you enter items into the cash book it is also useful to make a note of what they are.

If you take money out for your own use, or pay for something out of the business current account, then this will be recorded as *drawings*. Conversely, when you put your own money into the business, this should be recorded as *capital introduced*.

Expenditure January

Date	Chq no.	Payee	Amount	VAT	Goods	Rent / Rates / Insurance	Heat & Light	Tel.& Water	Advert Printing	Postage Stationery	Repairs Renewal	Wages	Drawing	Canteen	Prof Charges	Sundries
3	321	Salon Supplies	247.50	36.86	247.50											
3	322	British telecom	145.45	21.45				145.45								
4	323	London Gazette	75.45	11.24					75.45							
4	324	Chesham Dairies	10.34											10.34		
12	325	Clare Kemp	875.75									875.75				
12	326	James Coggan	1,024.15									1,024.15				
12	327	Karen Charles	425.55									425.55				
		Direct / Standing orders														
15		M Ford	1,200										1,200			
22		Co Op Bank	95.25												95.25	
28		Electricity Co.	141	21			141									
		Cash Payments														
		Petty cash/Draws	225										125	100		
		Totals	4,465.44	90.55	247.50	0	141	145.45	75.45	0	0	2,325.45	1,325	110.34	95.25	0

pre-printed accounting books

There are several variations of these systems on the market. The popular Collins simplex system has a separate page for each week and includes both bank and cash transactions as well as useful notes and guidance. The way that these systems are laid out may at first seem a little strange for your business, but with a bit of perseverance they can readily be adapted to suit your particular needs.

In the Collins system you will find space to record your daily sales and any other miscellaneous receipts at the top left. On the right-hand side there is space to record the money you have paid into the bank. Below this are a range of headings for the commonest types of expenses with additional blank lines for your own details. At the foot of the page there are spaces where you can summarise both your bank and cash transactions for the week.

cheque books, paying-in books and business cards

Business cheque books usually contain 50 cheques and are normally of a larger format than that used for personal cheques. Each cheque has a unique serial number so that accounting for them is simple; if your first cheque is numbered 10000 then the last in the book will be 100049. Unlike personal cheques, business cheques do not have a cheque guarantee card. This can often be a problem when you want to purchase items from firms that don't know you. The option of paying expenses by cheque is the simplest method of tracking your business current account. Always fill in the cheque stubs so that the cash book can be accurately updated at some later time. Banks tend to issue cheque books automatically when a particular serial number is processed. This can often lead to having several cheque books in hand at any one time. Make sure you look after all these cheque books to minimise their fraudulent use. Similarly, always check that you use the cheque books in consecutive order, so that your cash book will track the drafted cheques in the right order.

Only use the account paying-in book for making payments into the business account, to ensure that you have a complete financial record of all credits made.

Many firms now use a business credit card as a purchase card for their sundry purchases. In fact even your product manufacturers may offer this payment facility for the purchase of goods. This is fine if you pay promptly when the statements arrive. Otherwise it can be a very unwise move, as the accrued interest on large sums outstanding makes the purchase of goods in this way a very expensive option indeed.

cash payments

There will always be occasions where business expenses are paid in cash. This can make it difficult to track or keep account of such payments. The simplest way to record them is to pay these expenses out of your own pocket and then make out an expense voucher. At the end of the month, collect your receipts together and write a business cheque to yourself to cover your costs.

◼ managing VAT

Everyone comes into contact with VAT. We all pay it indirectly everyday. As a business manager it is highly unlikely that you will operate for very long before you will have to register for VAT. Only very small businesses turn over a gross figure beneath the VAT threshold. If you are starting out in business, make sure that you take VAT into consideration when pricing your services. Many small businesses fail because they do not appreciate that VAT has to be charged. This may seem to be a minor consideration, but the way that salons charge for their services on a simple tariff system hides the VAT portion within their prices. This is unlike all your suppliers, who invoice you for goods and then add the VAT on.

So, stressing the point, when you first open your business you must make sure that your prices accord with the market you are aiming at. As the business grows, you could soon attract VAT and then have to increase your prices by 17.5 per cent. Will your customers understand your predicament? Will they continue to come?

principle of VAT

VAT is based on what are known as 'output tax' and 'input tax'. If a business is registered for VAT, VAT output tax will be charged by you to your customers. Conversely, input tax is the VAT charged to you by your suppliers.

who collects VAT?

VAT is collected at every stage in the distribution of goods and services by taxable persons registered with Customs and Excise. The term 'taxable person' refers to the self-employed, partnerships, limited companies, clubs etc.

VAT registration

From 1st April 2000 you have to register for VAT if, in any month, the taxable supplies you have made in the past twelve months or less has exceeded £51,000; or there are reasonable grounds for believing that the value of the taxable supplies that will be made in the next 30 days will exceed £51,000.

Once registration has been made, VAT must be paid on all taxable outputs, i.e. the gross sales attained by the business. Conversely, VAT on all taxable inputs, i.e. the purchases made by the business in respect to stock, equipment and so on, may be reclaimed.

De-registration from VAT based upon expected turnover over the next 12 months has been raised to £49,000. For more information and/or leaflets, see Appendix 2.

how does VAT work?

The present VAT system ensures that each business becomes a collector of taxes. The current rate for VAT is 17.5 per cent, and is referred to as the *standard rate*. All transactions which attract VAT are called *taxable supplies*; VAT that you charge to your customers is called the *output tax*. In addition, the purchases made by the business in the day-to-day activities contain a VAT portion. This is called the *input tax*.

At the end of your VAT period you will have to settle up with H.M. Customs and Excise. If your total output tax on sales exceeds the total of input tax on your purchases, you must pay the difference to the VAT office.

VAT returns

In order for you to complete your VAT return, your records will need to show:

- The value of output tax on sales
- The value of input tax on purchases
- The amount of total sales excluding VAT
- The amount of total purchases excluding VAT.

Every three months you will be required to accumulate the figures over that period. Customs and Excise will send you a form VAT100 for your completion, and you must enter the necessary information and return the form with your cheque payment. Note that H.M. Customs and Excise do not provide additional copies of their forms, so make sure when you complete your return that you photocopy the **completed** form for your end-of-year accounts.

what if I don't pay VAT on time?

You must complete the VAT return and submit it to the VAT office within one month of the end of the VAT quarter. If you fail to make payment by the due date on your VAT return, regardless of whether it is late by an oversight or because you have not got the funds to pay it at that time, you will receive a Surcharge Liability Notice for VAT. When this is served on you it will state that you will be liable for a surcharge of 5 per cent. Each time you default, the penalty, i.e. your surcharge, goes up. This penalty remains in force until a full year has passed without default.

working out VAT

For businesses that are VAT registered, the difference between your gross sales and net sales will be the VAT portion.

The example on page 66 shows *gross* total sales of £3,039.28; this figure is inclusive of VAT. In order to work out the VAT within £3,039.28 we do the following sum:

Multiply 3,039.28 by 7 and then divide by 47 (this gives the VAT within a sum)
Hence 3,039.28 × 7 = 21,274.96 divided by 47 = 452.66

Working this back: if you take 3,039.28 − 452.66 the result is 2,586.62, the *net* daily sales. (Multiply this figure by 17.5 per cent and see the result!)

◼ your annual accounts

Every business manager needs to understand the year end accounts, so in this section we shall look at the way in which these accounts are prepared and drafted.

One of the main reasons for keeping the cash book and other records up-to-date is so that the year end accounts can be prepared, to show how the business is doing.

The prepared annual accounts consist of two main pages; an additional 'Notes to the accounts' provides a detailed breakdown for the reader.

There are many ways of setting out the annual accounts and the next three illustrations (which include an example of Notes to the Accounts) show the commonest layouts:

◼ The Balance Sheet
◼ The Profit and Loss Account.

The Balance Sheet provides the reader with a snapshot of the business assets and liabilities at a specific point in time. The term 'assets' refers to things that belong to the business; these could be monies deposited in bank accounts, people that owe the firm money (debtors), motor vehicles, stock in hand and all the salon equipment. Conversely, 'liabilities' refer to amounts owed by the business to other people (creditors). These could be loans, overdrafts, hire purchase agreements and things such as money owed for stock etc.

The year end accounts show these figures over one year's trading and, from this, anyone reading the accounts can see where and how monetary values have changed.

The Profit and Loss Account provides the reader with a reconciled summary of trading income and expenditure for a firm's completed financial year. Looking in isolation at just one year's accounts doesn't really provide a broad trading picture. So therefore when accounts are published, comparisons can be drawn by looking at columns showing two years' activity.

The illustration on page 72 provides an example of typical end of year accounts.

understanding accounts

The accounts contain information that can be analysed in many ways. The main indicators that denote the health of the business are:

gross profit margin

The gross profit is the profit sum derived from trading after allowing for direct costs (see page 74):
sales − cost of sales = gross profit.
The direct costs relate to staff wages and stock purchases. This sum is also commonly indicated as a percentage; by illustrating it in this way the ratio of profit to direct costs per £1 can be easily identified.

net profit margin

The net profit margin incorporates all the overhead costs and provides a final 'bottom line' figure on the Profit and Loss Account. This is often written as a percentage in respect to turnover, but is not as important as the gross profit figure.

As general guidance, we can now look at some ideal operating ranges:

1. A good business should be generating a gross profit of 45 to 58 per cent.

2. Ideally, purchases of consumables should not exceed 10 per cent of turnover; if you find that your stock is significantly higher than this, negotiate for better deals. It is also worth making allowances for salons that purchase heavily for retailing.

3. Salaries for staff should not exceed 50 per cent of turnover.

J.P. Arnold
Balance Sheet as at 9th May 2000

		2000 £	1999 £
Fixed Assets	1.	7543	6995
Current Assets	2.		
Stock		3400	2100
Debtors and prepayments		540	480
Cash in hand		798	1000
Bank balance		2275	1790
		7013	5370
Current liabilities			
Creditors and accruals		4222	4762
Net current assets/ (liabilities)		2791	608
Net assets		10334	7603
Financed by :			
Capital account	3.	10334	7603

Approved ....
J.P. Arnold

Date ....

J.P. Arnold
PROFIT AND LOSS ACCOUNT
FOR THE YEAR ENDED 9th MAY 2000

	2000	1999
Sales	86442	69888
Cost of Sales	35600	29800
Gross Profit	58.81% 50842	57.36% 40088
Operating Expenses	26700	21500
Profit for the year transferred to Capital account	24142	18588

J.P. Arnold
NOTES TO THE ACCOUNTS for the year ended 9th May 2000

	2000	1999
1. Cost of Sales		
Wages	25140	21800
Purchases	11760	8500
Stock at beginning of year	2100	1600
Stock at end of year	(3400)	(2100)
	35600	29800
2. Operating Expenses		
Premises expenses		
Rent	4000	4000
Rates	1848	1675
Light and heat	1600	1450
	7448	7125

	2000	1999
Repairs and renewals	784	875
General expenses		
Printing, stationery, advertising	5750	3750
Post and telephone	647	560
Insurances	970	825
Sundries	2657	1890
Motor expenses	1750	1050
Legal and Professional	840	680
Accountancy and book-keeping	875	785
Depreciation	785	700
Finance expenses		
Bank charges	2050	1975
Training	2144	1285
	26700	21500

3. Capital Account

Beginning of year	7603
Capital introduced	3589
Profit for year	24142
Drawings	(25000)
Balance at end of year	10334

4. Fixed Assets

	Total	Motor vehicle	Fixture/fittings
Written down value at 10\5\99	6995	1800	5195
Additions	1333		1333
Depreciation	(785)	(450)	(335)
Written down values at 9\5\00	7543	1350	6193

capital expenditure and revenue expenditure

There are two types of expenditure that are made by the business. Capital expenditure refers to the purchases of fixed assets, such as salon equipment, which will be used by the business for several years. Revenue expenditure refers to purchases that, over a shorter term, will be used in the generation of profits, such as stock.

balance sheet

The Balance Sheet sets out the total assets and liabilities for the business at a set point in time. The information held here will highlight the strengths or weaknesses of the business and will cover the following aspects.

fixed assets

This relates to property, fixtures, fittings and vehicles, as these major items are of long-lasting benefit to the business.

current assets

Unlike fixed assets, these have a short-term benefit to the business and will encompass items such as stock in hand, money on deposit in the bank, and people that owe you money (i.e. debtors).

current liabilities

This term refers to those that you owe money to. Your creditors could be the bank, by means of an overdraft, or suppliers of stock received but not yet paid for.

net current assets (liabilities)

The net current assets are the difference between the current assets and the current liabilities, often referred to as *working capital*. This is the day-to-day value available to the business for its day-to-day running. When current assets exceed current liabilities, the resultant figure becomes a net current asset; conversely, when current assets are exceeded by current liabilities, a resultant net current liability is shown.

net assets

This is arrived at by adding the fixed assets to the net current assets (liabilities). This figure shows the total net worth of the business.

capital account (proprietor's investment)

At the bottom of the Balance Sheet shown on page 71 we can see that the net assets are matched with an equal figure. This sum represents the capital account or in other words the proprietor's investment in the business. This could reflect either profits earned by the business and not taken out, or money invested in the business. In simple terms, if all the assets were realised and liabilities repaid, then this sum would be left for the business to pay over to its owner.

profit and loss account

The Balance Sheet provides a financial picture of the business at a fixed point in time. The Profit and Loss Account, in contrast, shows the sales generated by the business, the costs of those sales and a gross profit figure from which the operating expenses are deducted, which in turn provides a resultant net profit over the accounting period.

gross profit

This is the value derived from deducting the cost of sales, i.e. the total salaries and stock purchases (including stock in hand at beginning of year and stock in hand at end of year), from the overall trading sales figures. The figure may be illustrated in two ways, as a percentage and as sum value.

net profit

The net profit for the year, which is transferred to the capital account, is derived by deducting the operating expenses (the expenditure in respect of the overhead) from the gross profit.

notes to the accounts

The notes to the accounts provide a detailed summary or financial breakdown. In the Notes to the Accounts on pages 72 and 73 we can see that section 1 (Cost of Sales) contains values for wages, purchases and stock in hand. Section 2 provides a detailed break-down of operational costs. Section 3 illustrates the proprietor's financial stake in the business within the capital account. Finally, Section 4 itemises the fixed assets and their subsequent depreciation.

depreciation

Capital items, i.e. fixed assets bought by the business (such as equipment or vehicles), have a long but limited life span. Over the years these items lose their value and the accounts must reflect this. To cover this aspect, allowances are made which 'write off' part of the value each year as an expense of the business. This is called depreciation. As it would be unrealistic to have valuers come in and provide a written-down value each year, a notional figure is used to transfer from the asset account and treat as an expense in the Profit and Loss Account as a fixed percentage each year.

■ budgeting and cash flow forecasting

We previously looked at the business annual accounts, a snapshot of business activity over a set period in time. This provided us with an historical view of what had happened before. We now want to predict the future! We can only do this by budgeting and fore-casting. By forecasting the income and expenditure of the business, we can forecast the Balance Sheet to show the financial health of the business in twelve months' time.

In creating a detailed plan for budgets, you will need to remember the proportional links that exist between the financial variables. For example

Sales budget ======== Cost of sales

When you set your sales budget, you will need to con-sider the cost of sales. If you cast your mind back to accounts, you will remember that cost of sales refers to wages and purchases. If you expect to achieve higher sales, what will be the cost of achieving those

sales? Will it still be profitable with those increased costs?

In a similar way

Overheads ======== Sales budget

Your business overheads will be incurred whatever the level of sales achieved. However, as sales increase, the proportion of overhead costs reduces per service provided.

The next two illustrations show how these costs affect the business, and how overheads effectively decrease as sales increase.

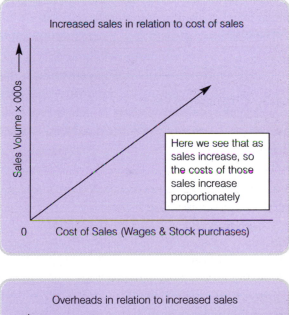

Increased sales in relation to cost of sales

Sales Volume × 000s

Here we see that as sales increase, so the costs of those sales increase proportionately

0   Cost of Sales (Wages & Stock purchases)

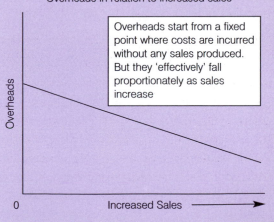

Overheads in relation to increased sales

Overheads

Overheads start from a fixed point where costs are incurred without any sales produced. But they 'effectively' fall proportionately as sales increase

0   Increased Sales

cash flow forecasts

Cash flow projections are an essential tool for every-day use within your business, as well as being a core component for initial business planning. Computing has made this task much simpler in recent years. All office type software packages contain worksheet facilities and simple cash flows can be created within minutes.

In the past, figures were broken down more or less in line with the annual audit, which would have given a broader overview and certainly wouldn't have given specific details about the critical periods within the year when major cash outgoings occurred. Therefore, in recent years cash flow projections have been given much closer scrutiny and analysis.

The figure below gives an example cash flow fore-cast.

In this example we see the critical periods facing the business; as VAT payments are made, the bank account 'plunges' dramatically. In July a previously accumulating account of £3,310 is reduced to £620.

Here, again, a balance that is in credit is turned into an overdraft for two months, during January and February.

When arranging overdraft facilities with your bank, these periods must be taken into consideration. It is all-too-easy to lose business credibility when having to request an additional short-term loan because the business is facing unexpected financial difficulties. In recent years, bank managers have not been very help-ful to small businesses that are not able to present accurate financial information.

Accuracy is imperative – everything falls back on your ability to forecast, although it is worth remember-ing that trends and patterns can change.

When you devise a cash flow projection it will pro-vide you with a good measure for the business. If you are asked by your bank to produce one, ensure that you present figures that are realistic and relate to the business, not just figures drafted to please the bank manager.

	May	Jun.	Jul.	Aug.	Sep.	Oct.	Nov.	Dec.	Jan.	Feb.	Mar.	Apr.	TOTAL
Income A	11,400	10,100	9,850	10,750	11,000	8,250	8,450	13,000	9,000	9,250	11,500	13,500	126,050
Salaries	4,000	4,000	4,000	4,000	4,000	4,000	4,000	5,000	4,000	4,000	4,500	4,500	50,000
Purchase	1,050	1,000	1,020	1,500	950	900	950	1,750	1,000	970	1,050	1,500	13,640
Overhds	3,070	3,070	3,070	3,070	3,070	3,070	3,070	3,070	3,070	3,070	3,070	3,070	36,840
Rent		1,500			1,500			1,500			1,500		6,000
Loans	250	250	250	250	250	250	250	250	250	250	250	250	3,000
Total pmnts B	8,370	9,820	8,340	8,820	9,770	8,220	8,270	11,570	8,320	8,290	10,370	9,320	107,980
VAT pyb			4,200			3,744			4,000			4,579	16,523
monthly figs A–B	3,030	280	−2,690	1,930	1,230	−3,714	180	1,430	−3,320	960	1,130	−399	
Bank A/C	3,030	3,310	620	2,550	3,780	66	246	1,676	−1,644	−684	446	47	

When these projections are used properly, they will quickly identify the various problems within the business so that immediate action can be taken to remedy the situation.

Always refer to your projections on a monthly basis so that actual figures can be assessed against predictions. This can easily be monitored by introducing two columns per month, one being a projection and the other being actual (see page 78). If this is updated regularly it will settle into a pattern and provide an indication of the firm's future capital needs. Always remember to include every item of expenditure and build in a margin for error by adding, say, 10 per cent. This can also be applied to the total receipts by taking a fairly average turnover and reducing it by the same margin.

Receipts	Month Budget	Jan. Actual	Month Budget	Feb. Actual	Month Budget	Mar. Actual
Cash Sales	780	771	850	873	850	781
Capital Introduced	950	950				
Total Receipts A	1,730	1,721	850	873	850	781
Payments						
Creditors			51	31	51	53
Cash Purchases	51	83	51	48	51	52
Rent/Rates	22	22	22	22	22	22
Insurances	300	300				
Repairs/ Renewals	12	0	12	0	12	0
Electricity					15	15
Advertising	100	115				
Print/Stationery			5	11	5	4
Motor	30	32	30	43	130	157
Telephone					20	20
Professional fees			50	50	50	50
Capital Payments	875	875				
Drawings	420	420	420	420	420	420
Sundries	150	150				
Total Payments B	1,960	1,997	641	625	776	793
A – B Cash Flow	−230	−276	209	248	74	−12
Opening Balance	Nil	Nil	−230	−276	−21	−28
Closing Balance	−230	−276	−21	−28	53	−40

Business manager's checklist

Activity to Check	Daily	Weekly	Monthly	Quarterly
Check takings against till	✓			
Complete daily records	✓			
Bank Money, Cheques etc	✓			
Check incoming goods	✓			
Check stock in hand		✓		
Complete weekly records		✓		
Reconcile the bank A/C		✓		
Complete the cash book			✓	
Pay Wages and complete wages book			✓	
Update cash flow forecast			✓	
Pay VAT				✓
Review income and expenditure				✓

5 employment

part 5

employment

81

recruitment and selection

summary

Attracting the right people and making effective use of them is an essential part of creating a successful business formula. Getting staff levels right can be a difficult exercise, not only for staff numbers, but also for the mix of abilities (i.e. technical skills). Each member of staff will have differing strengths and weaknesses, and good management relies upon the continuation of further development in weak areas, whilst capitalising on the stronger aspects. We should not only be looking at the number of staff employed but also the mix of ability, or potential ability, which will enable the business to compete.

Acquiring the right person for the job is not a simple task and should not be taken lightly, so in this part of the book we shall first look at how staff appointment should be addressed. This process includes the following necessary considerations:

- Job analysis
- Description of duties (Job description)
- The person specification
- Advertising the post
- Short listing
- Interviewing
- Making the job offer.

evaluating staff requirement

Consider the following questions:

1. Do we have sufficient business to warrant a new appointment?
2. Do we need to replace a member of staff who is leaving?
3. Has the nature of the job changed since the last appointment?
4. Could changes to existing job roles satisfy business needs more effectively?

job analysis

When a decision has been made either to create a new job or to replace an existing one, a clear understanding of the job role needs to be evaluated so that a true profile, i.e. Job description, can be drafted. Job analysis involves a close study of all aspects relating to the job. This can be achieved by:

- Observing the tasks and duties relating to the job
- Discussion with others who perform similar roles
- Reviewing records relating to staff, appraisals and training.

In drafting a description of the job you should consider the following:

Questions to consider for Job analysis

What is the Job title?

What is the Job's main purpose?

What are the responsibilities and to whom will the person appointed be accountable?

What tasks and skills are involved?

What are the physical and/or mental demands?

What are the working conditions?

job description

After analysing the job, it should be possible to draw up a description which will specify the job's

- Purpose
- Duties
- Relationships.

A well-drafted job description provides management with a profile for the person specification, a basis from which application forms and adverts can be generated, and the framework for performance appraisal.

In the two sample job descriptions that follow, sometimes standards of behaviour and appearance are included; if these are included from the outset, the job holder will know exactly what is expected of them.

Job Description – Stylist
Job Title: Stylist
Location: Based at salon as advised

Main purpose of job:	To ensure customer care is provided at all times
	To rnaintain a good standard of technical and client care, ensuring that up-to-date methods and techniques are used that follow the salon training practices and procedures.
Responsible to:	Salon manager
Requirements:	To maintain the Company's standards in respect of hairdressing//beauty services
	To ensure that all clients receive the best possible quality service
	To advise clients on services and treatments
	To advise clients on products and after care
	To achieve designated performance targets
	To participate in self-development or to assist with the development of others
	To maintain Company policy in respect of:

a)   Personal standards of health and hygiene
b)   Personal standards of appearance and conduct
c)   Operating safely whilst at work
d)   Public promotion
e)   Corporate image as laid out in employee handbook

To carry out client consultation in accordance with Company policy

To maintain Company security practices and procedures

To assist your manager in the provision of salon resources

To undertake additional tasks and duties required by your manager from time to time.

Conditions of service:	35 hour week – Flexible Rostering between Monday and Saturday, 9.00 am to 5.30 pm.
	1 hour lunch break. 20 days' annual leave. Salary band F, £8950 to £12,400.

Job Description – Salon Manager
Job Title: Manager
Location: Based at salon as advised

Main purpose:	Responsible for salon efficiency and job profitability whilst ensuring that Company standards are maintained in respect of:

a)   Financial/productivity targets
b)   Technical standards
c)   Quality service
d)   Corporate image requirements
e)   Salon procedures.

Responsible to: General manager

Responsibilities: Financial/productivity targets

To achieve pre-defined sales targets

To ensure staff provide quality service

To oversee reception procedures whilst maintaining financial responsibility

To monitor accuracy in respect of company records and documentation.

Technical standards:

To liaise with Training Manager to provide information for developmental activities

To monitor standards of service provision

To monitor and review customer service expectations

To develop and maintain after care services/sales support.

Client care:

To implement approved consultation systems

To handle customer complaints in line with company customer care policy.

Staff management:

To motivate and guide staff members

To establish and maintain a harmonious working environment

To facilitate staff in the promotion of quality service standards

To establish effective lines of communication

To ensure that grievance procedures are effected according to Company policy

To ensure that disciplinary procedures are effected according to Company policy.

Image standards:

To ensure that expected standards of personal hygiene and appearance are maintained

To ensure standards of salon cleanliness and hygiene are maintained

To carry out all reasonable duties and tasks as requested.

Conditions of service: 38 hour week – Monday to Saturday (variable day off), 8.30 am to 5.30 pm. 20 days' annual leave.

Salary band M, £15,600 to £18,200.

person specification

It is very easy to make mistakes in the selection of staff, often because there is no clear idea about the person required. Drawing up a profile of the expected job holder will dispense with misconceptions. This type of profile is called a *person specification* and is the logical progression following on from the job analysis and the job description. A good person specification will be able to: state what it is that is being looked for in job applicants; provide essential criteria that will facilitate the selection process; and provide equal opportunities and accessibility to prospective candidates.

When you draft a person specification, there are simple guidelines that you can follow:

1. Don't use sketchy terms when looking for essential requirements, i.e. good all-round ability required.

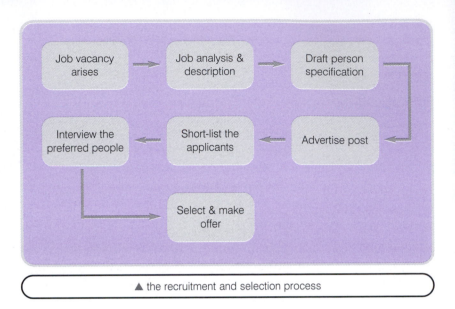

▲ the recruitment and selection process

2. Don't use vagaries in reference to the required personal qualities, such as 'good communicator' or 'bright and breezy personality'.

3. Be realistic with expectations; if you set your sights too high you may eliminate perfectly good candidates.

4. Never discriminate between different groups on the grounds of nationality, age or sex. See employment legislation on page 105.

The Job Holder
(List the necessary criteria under the following headings)

Attainments

These should state the minimum criteria expected from the Job Holder and will cover qualifications, training, previous experience as well as skills and knowledge.

Abilities

These are the talents and aptitudes that you would expect the Job Holder to be capable of, and these may include level of general intelligence.

Personal circumstances

Will the candidate need to live within a particular area? Is there any need for working unusual hours? Do they need a driving licence?

a model for drafting a person specification

To assist in the selection process it is particularly helpful to identify which qualities are essential (i.e. the required qualities which absence of in a person would eliminate that person from the selection process) and those that are merely desirable (i.e. qualities that could be otherwise attained through training or be compensated for in some other way).

A checklist for identifying the right candidate
(based upon the Dr. Alec Rodger's seven point plan)

Physical characteristics:

Personal health and fitness
Appearance and personal hygiene
First impressions

Attainments:

Educational achievement, GCSEs, GNVQs, A levels or AS levels
Vocational achievement, NVQs, technical courses attended, apprenticeship
Vocational experience

General intelligence:

Common sense
Ability to learn quickly
Good memory

Aptitudes:

Creative or artistic ability
Manual manipulation and dexterity
Natural ability with figures, computing
Communication skills

Interests:

Artistic, literary
Social, sporting

Disposition:

Acceptability to others, responsible, leadership

Circumstances:

Family dependency, work flexibility, travel requirements

looking to future employment needs

Having made the decision to recruit staff, don't just consider the immediate or short-term requirements, look to the future. If, for example, you are looking for an experienced operator and you anticipate the existing salon manager is likely to emigrate in 18 months time leaving you without any suitable replacement, perhaps you should consider recruiting someone who will not only be a good stylist now but would be a possible replacement when the existing salon manager leaves.

planning for future employment needs: questions for consideration

the workforce

1. What skills, experience and aptitudes do your existing staff provide?
2. What are their ages?
3. Do you expect any moves towards part-time or even resignations?
4. Are your employees flexible in relation to working hours/days?

the business plan

1. Do you intend to expand the business (by providing additional services or treatments etc.)?
2. Do you envisage any changes, moves or even a re-location?
3. Do you expect the business to contract?
4. Are you going to operate a seven-day provision of service?

external factors

1. Is there any demographic downturn that would provide fewer school leavers?
2. Are young people staying on for further education?
3. Is there a growing market for women returners?
4. How will government policies and initiatives affect or influence your business?

application forms

A well-drafted application form will channel the information required from the applicants in order to assist in the selection process. This in turn will help you to:

- Focus on only the required information
- Standardise the quality of the required information
- Promote and enhance the business image
- Create a 'bank' of future prospective candidates
- Assess individual responses to specific or technical questions.

Whether you choose to use application forms or not is up to you. Forms can, however, be adapted to cover specific posts (for example, specific or technical questions could be included to relate to particular jobs).

curriculum vitae

Some employers prefer applicants to submit their Curriculum Vitae (C.V.) as an initial means of selection. As an employer, you should be able to establish from a well-drafted C.V. the candidate's aptitude for the job, level of motivation and ability to fit in. In many cases, employers will use the contents of the C.V. as the basis for the job interview. This type of personal profile has particular advantages, although there is a drawback.

advantages

- A well-drafted C.V. will provide adequate background information about the candidate in logical order
- The C.V.'s format will provide the reader with the applicant's organisational and presentation skills (if prepared by the candidate!)
- It is quick and easy to cross-reference to the person specification.

disadvantage

- Many people do not know how to structure a C.V. This may allow perfectly good candidates to slip through the selection process.

Dos and Don'ts when preparing a Curriculum Vitae

Do:	Don't:
Tailor the C.V. and covering letter to match the job requirement.	Present your information poorly.
Research the company/firm that you hope to work for so that you can personalise your application.	Produce over-long documents (2 pages of A4 maximum).
Focus on what you have to offer in the future, not just what you have achieved in the past.	Make typographical or grammatical errors.
Address your C.V. directly to your recipient, avoiding 'Dear Sir'	Be disorganised with your content and information.

advertising the post

Assuming that you are going to advertise the job vacancy externally, there are a number of considerations that must be taken into account – primarily, what medium you will use and what the advantages and disadvantages are. The options for communicating your vacancy may be grouped into the following types:

- Personal communication
- Press, i.e. newspapers, magazines, periodicals etc.
- Employment or careers agency
- Training providers
- Salon display.

personal communication

Making personal contact by approaching prospective candidates directly has a number of advantages. You have already identified your 'ideal' employee. This may be because they have previously worked for you and you are therefore aware of the quality of their performance and skill. They could have been recommended to you by other members of staff or clients. Obviously this method of recruitment benefits from being very inexpensive.

However, a possible candidate may be known to you because of their standing or reputation as a competitor; this is the darker side of personal contact and is generally known as 'poaching'. Resorting to this form of recruitment will not improve your professional standing within your local community.

press

This medium for communication can be utilised on either a local or national basis and will depend on the nature of the job. For example, a large salon group with outlets in major department stores in larger cities throughout the country may find that national advertising in newspapers or trade publications suits their recruitment needs better; whereas a smaller independent firm located in a provincial area may only want to access suitable applicants within the immediate locality. The main advantage of using this medium is that the expected response will be swift, however companies that use the national press may find this

option expensive, particularly if 'display' advertising is used, as commercially designed artwork and copy details can involve high professional labour costs.

employment agencies/careers agencies and JobCentres

The main advantage of using a personnel recruitment firm is that they will carry out the preliminary selection for you in line with your selection criteria. Their service will provide you with a short list of suitable candidates ready for interview. This method may seem attractive but can be expensive. However, making your needs known to schools via the County Careers Service can prove an inexpensive way of accessing a large number of potential candidates, particularly for positions such as trainees, apprentices etc.

JobCentres provide a free recruitment service and are located in many town high streets. Staff take the details of your job vacancy and advertise the vacancy on their notice boards, and they will, if required, circulate the information to other JobCentres. When job seekers enquire for further details, the centres' staff will contact you immediately or, if you prefer, they will issue the applicant with an application form and draw up a provisional short list for you.

training providers

This source of supply can be an effective solution, particularly when looking for candidates that are undergoing specific training or are near completion of training. The training providers may be local colleges, the local authorities or independent training organisations. This may provide a suitable option, especially when looking for inexperienced staff, as all training providers are responsible for delivering training to at least the national minimum standards.

salon display

This can be a very cheap way to advertise your employment needs – a poster in the salon window could catch the attention of many passers-by, but it may take sometime before the word gets around and suitable applicants come forward.

recruitment checklist – sources of supply

Source	Advantages	Disadvantages	Costs
Personal contact	Could be quick/convenient; could be friends of existing staff; could help morale	Friends may not be the most suitable candidates	Free
Schools/Colleges	Good regular supply	Probably little experience; will need training	Free
JobCentres	Wide coverage	Centre staff may suggest unsuitable people; only people looking for work apply, as opposed to people already within employment	Free
Employment Agencies	Good for locating specialists; good pre-selection	Expensive	High
Press (newspapers etc.)	Good coverage (local, national); quick to publish; trade journals target specific interested groups	Adverts could be missed because of poor positioning of inserts; short 'life span'	Local: low/medium National: high
Salon display	Quick to produce; attract local attention	May take time for word to get around	Low

advertising vacancies

When you have decided which recruitment method you wish to use, you must think carefully about the way the vacancy should be advertised. Consider: What information should be put in the advert? How should that information be phrased? How should the advert be designed? It is essential that you can answer these questions if you intend to draft your own adverts.

Before planning your advert, you should be aware of other people's adverts: What details do they include or exclude, and in what way do they put those details across? Which of the adverts do you think readers would respond to, and why?

In radio advertising it is important not only to talk to but also to be guided by the radio station's professional staff. By all means provide information and suggestions, but this medium is so specialised that an amateur, however gifted, is unlikely to be able to plan and produce a good advert on their own.

The contents of an advert will always vary according to circumstances. For example, a display advert in a local newspaper may allow you more room than a notice in a JobCentre window. However, you would usually seek to include some, or even all, of the following details:

- The job title
- The job location

- Information about the business – the products you sell, the manufacturers you use and the services you provide
- Information about the job – its purpose and main tasks
- The job benefits – any benefits which will encourage people to apply for the job
- The salary – always state the precise salary or possible range
- The type of person required – the skills, qualifications and experience that the right person must have
- Who to apply to – yourself, a colleague or a subordinate
- Where to apply
- How to apply – whether by application form, Curriculum Vitae, letter or telephone.

short listing

This is the next stage in the process. When the applicants have responded to the advert and completed and returned the application forms, the information should be evaluated against the person specification so that a suitable short list can be drawn up.

The drafted short list identifies the candidates who:

- Meet most or all of the requirements
- Meet some requirements but could be developed further to meet more of them.

interviewing and selection

The purpose of interviewing is to assess the suitability of each of the short-listed candidates for the job vacancy. However, to reach this aim you will need to prepare yourself by careful planning, which will involve:

- Choosing a suitable time for the interviews to take place
- Selecting who should be present
- Deciding how applicants should be received
- Structuring the interview (what questions etc.).

The time and duration of interviews will depend on the time-scale allowed for the recruitment phase. The amount of time allocated for each interview will depend on the type of vacancy that exists, but in all situations should provide adequate time to allow:

- All parties to indicate whether they can attend
- Interviewer(s) to elicit sufficient information on which a decision can be based
- Applicants to 'state their case'
- Adequate assessment of each candidate between appointments.

Arrangements will need to be made for receiving and welcoming candidates in comfortable surroundings while awaiting their interview. The interview location should be free of interruptions and be comfortable in terms of heating, ventilation and seating. Particular attention should be given to the arrangement of furniture within the interview room, as this will affect the interview 'atmosphere'.

The various furniture arrangements used in interview rooms will influence the psychological formality of the process (see the illustration below).

In the illustration, a 'hatched' circle represents the applicant. In the first and third diagram, there is a desk

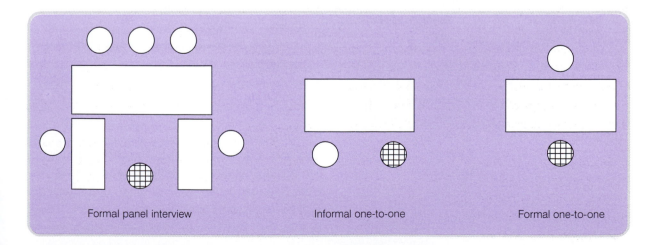

Formal panel interview   Informal one-to-one   Formal one-to-one

between the interviewer(s) and interviewee which creates a psychological barrier and will maintain a formal atmosphere. However, the central diagram shows both parties, interviewer and interviewee side by side, and this will create a far less formal, almost relaxed atmosphere.

the panel interview

This type of interview method is becoming increasingly popular. In small businesses the panel could comprise yourself, the successful candidate's immediate superior and a member of staff in a similar technical role (so that specific technical knowledge could be accurately evaluated).

Advantages	Disadvantages
Fairer, unbiased and more accurate method of assessment	It can be quite daunting for the candidate to face several interviewers
Interviewers share the questioning responsibility and selection decision	It could be difficult to get everyone to attend
It appears more professional	
Easier to take notes without interrupting the flow	

the one-to-one interview

As shown in the illustration above, a one-to-one interview can be either a formal or an informal situation, and will rely solely on the interviewer's skills.

Advantages	Disadvantages
Easy to arrange at mutually convenient time	Your assessment may be unreliable
The candidate will feel more relaxed facing only one interviewer	You could be a poor interviewer
It is easier for the interviewer to 'steer' and control the conversation	You may lack experience in interviewing and find it difficult to reach a decision

asking the right questions

To make best use of the interview time, you must have prepared relevant questions. For interviewing purposes there are four main categories:

- Closed questions
- Open questions
- Probing questions
- Problem-centred questions.

closed questions

This type of question is only concerned with a single fact, or merely invites the answer 'yes' or 'no'. They do not encourage the responder to expand on their answer. Examples of such questions are:

1. Have you had experience with appointment scheduling?
2. Where did you train previously?
3. Where did you see our advert?

Closed questions are useful if you only want to check information, but they tend to close off two-way communication unless they are followed up with another question.

open questions

Open questions invite the interviewee to produce a full and complete reply to the question being asked. They therefore give the interviewer a much better opportunity to assess the applicant's personality, experience, knowledge and general suitability. Because these questions open up the interview, they require more input from the candidate and less from the interviewer. Examples of such questions are:

1. Tell me about the types of treatment you provided in your previous job?
2. What areas did you cover when you attended the academy course?

probing questions

This type of question seeks to find out more information about what a candidate has already said. It provides the candidate with another opportunity to expand or illustrate their answer more fully. It also enables the interviewer to delve deeper into a specific subject, possibly to validate or verify what has previously been stated. Examples of such questions are:

1. What particular aspect of your last job did you not like?
2. Could you tell me the procedures that you carried out in respect of cashing up the till?

problem-centred questions

These questions are specifically designed to assess the response from a candidate under particular circumstances or in specific situations. This type of question will show how the candidate would deal with a particular problem. Examples of such questions are:

1. If a client was dissatisfied with the service you provided how would go about resolving the situation?
2. If a member of staff under your management had particularly low retail sales over the appraisal period how would you tackle the situation?

conducting the interview

The interviewer will take the predominant role at the beginning and the end of the interview, by opening the conversation, providing the candidate with information and finally bringing the interview to a close. But in a good interview it is the candidate who will do most of the talking.

keep an open mind

Never make a quick decision in the first few minutes based on the interviewee's speech, posture or mannerisms. Appearances can be deceptive, so give the candidate your attention throughout the interview. Give a fair hearing and at all costs avoid discrimination.

Allow the information to flow – let the candidate have sufficient time to respond to your questions, but avoid talking too much yourself. How will you be able to assess the candidate's suitability for the job unless most of the input comes from them. Encourage the candidate to talk through the use of open questions unless you are checking information from their application form.

appear interested

Show your readiness to listen through your posture, and by looking interested in a non-threatening way.

Indicate your attentiveness and encourage the candidate through nods, phrases such as 'go on ... tell me more ...', and appropriate facial expressions.

direct the conversation

Conversely, give the interviewee signals if they have said enough on a subject or if the response has wandered; steer the response back on course to elicit the desired information by comments such as 'can we come back to' or 'tell me more about'.

summarise

Summarise the interview content from time to time; this will ensure that your understanding of the facts is correct, and will give the opportunity to clarify details before going on.

take notes

You cannot expect to remember everything about each candidate, so take notes. Try to keep this unobtrusive as the interviewee may be put off by the interrupted flow of the interview. Don't write down detrimental information immediately it becomes apparent, as this may affect the confidence of the interviewee and could 'taint' the interview as a whole.

When the interview has revealed the information needed to assess the candidate properly, it can be brought to a close. Give the candidate the opportunity to put forward any questions they may have, making sure that you provide full and honest answers. It is important that all parties involved know exactly what is involved. Do not make an offer of the job at this stage even if you are certain that this is the ideal person, a subsequent interview may identify a more suitable candidate. Thank the applicant for attending and tell them that you will be in touch within the next few days. You can then signal that the interview is over by standing up and offering your hand before showing them to the door.

making a decision

The interviewer or panel should spend some time between interviews in reflecting on what has occurred in the previous interview, and make some assessment of the candidate's responses matched against the expected criteria. It could be helpful to fill out an interview assessment checklist in order to focus on the essential and desirable qualities that the candidate has to offer.

making a job offer

The successful candidate would normally be offered the job verbally, this usually being subject to satisfactory references being taken up. Sometimes suitable candidates decline to take up the offer, perhaps deciding that the job is not for them. Then 'second line' alternative choices can be approached. The final stage following acceptable responses from referees would be to prepare a formal letter stating the full details of the terms and conditions of the post and sending it to the applicant.

put it into writing

It is quite common for people to accept a job before receiving written confirmation. In fact, in many cases people never receive written particulars of their employment. This does not mean that they have no employee rights however; an inferred contract, enforceable in law between employer and employee, naturally comes into being. In order to avoid any conjecture or speculation, the terms of the job offer should be put into writing.

Notice period	It would normally not be in the employer's interest to grant a long notice period. See page 98, for employee statutory rights
Perks and Benefits	Do you offer a company car scheme? Who is responsible for car condition? Is there a fuel allowance?
	Do you offer a private medical scheme?
	Is there any occupational pension scheme?
Work locations	Do you need staff to be flexible in their place of work, and is this reasonable?
Confidentiality clauses	Is the nature of the work confidential? Will confidentiality need to be adhered to during and after employment?
Restrictive covenants	These have become more popular again in recent years. Will you require restrictions with regard to 'poaching' or working radius, should an employee leave?
Description of duties	Are descriptions of duties to be provided at the interview stage or afterwards?
Salary bonuses/commissions	Is your pay scheme easily understood? Does it relate to basic pay plus commission, or is it performance related in other ways?

▲ considerations for employers regarding terms of employment

contracts of employment

A contract of employment exists when an employee starts work, therefore by default he accepts the terms and conditions that have been offered. These terms and conditions may be provided in writing at the interview stage or based upon verbal comments made during the interview.

Drawing up a contract

When drafting a contract of employment, employers should seek legal advice if they wish to incorporate complex clauses or restrictive covenants.

The following contract is of a typical format that would be issued to employees in accordance with section 1 of the **Employment Rights Act 1996**.

Contract of Employment

This contract is made on <date> between:

    1) Head Quarters (a company registered in England & Wales)
       no. _____ of <address> ('We', 'Us' or the 'company')
    2) Hayley Smith of <address> ('You')

a)   Job title
We will employ you and you will work for us as a Salon manager/senior stylist.

b)   Commencement of employment
Your employment will begin on <date>.

c)   Location
Your normal place of work will be at our premises at <address> but we reserve the right to change such a place within the United Kingdom as we may reasonably require.

d)   Hours of work
Your normal working week will be Monday to Friday <times>. You are also be required to work additional hours as necessary for the performance of your duties.

e)   Pay
Your salary is <£XX,000> per annum payable monthly in arrears by direct transfer to your bank account on <xxth> of each month.

f)   Holidays
The holiday year runs from 1 January to 31 December. In addition to bank and other public holidays, the holiday entitlement is 15 days per annum, three of which must be taken between Christmas and New Year. If you start or leave your employment during the holiday year, your holiday entitlement for that year will be calculated on a pro rata basis. No holiday may be carried over from one holiday year to the next. No payment will be made in lieu of holiday accrued and not taken except in the year when you leave our employment.

g)   Sickness and injury
The company does not provide sickness pay. This does not affect your statutory rights regarding statutory sickness pay.

h)   Medical examinations
We reserve the right to ask you to be medically examined by a doctor of our choice at our expense. In addition, a medical questionnaire is enclosed which must be returned to our company doctor within five working days of your receiving this contract, using the enclosed self addressed envelope.

i)   Notice and trial period
Your employment will initially be for a trial period of three months. During your trial period we or you may terminate the employment by one week's notice in writing. If your employment is confirmed at the end of your trial period, the period of notice to be given in writing by you to us or by us to you to terminate your employment shall be not less than one month.

j)   Confidentiality
You must not at any time during (except in the course of your duties) or after your employment disclose or make use of your knowledge of any of our confidential information. Confidential information includes, without limitation, all and any information about business plans, maturing new business opportunities, know-how, sales statistics, marketing surveys and plans, costs, profit or loss, the names, addresses and contact details of customers which we treat as confidential.

k)   Disciplinary/grievance procedures
If you are dissatisfied with any disciplinary decision relating to you, or have a grievance about your employment, you should bring it to the attention of your line manager and/or human resources department as appropriate and, if you wish, the union representative. Please note that your right to be represented does not apply during your trial period. A full copy of the disciplinary rules and grievance procedure is set out in the company handbook.

Signed on behalf of Head Quarters

signed ....

position ....

signed .... (Hayley Smith)

rights and obligations at work

Even in the absence of a written job contract, the employer and employee are bound to each other by an array of legislatory statutes and common law. This protection for employees covers every step of employment from the submission of a C.V. to the receipt of a P45. No individual may be discriminated against on the basis of race, sex or disability. In addition to this overarching principle, the **Employment Rights Act 1996** provide the employee with additional safeguards. The most important of these are the right to:

- an itemised pay slip
- not be unfairly dismissed
- receive written reasons for dismissal
- receive and provide a minimum period of notice
- statutory maternity pay and maternity leave
- statutory sickness pay
- a statement of particulars of employment.

what new employees must be told in writing

Under the Employment's Rights Act 1996, all employees must receive a Statement of Particulars. All contracts of employment (see pages 95–96) should provide this information:

- names of employer and employee
- name and address of place of work
- date of which employment began
- date of which continuous employment began
- job title
- salary and payment interval (monthly or weekly)
- terms and conditions relating to hours of work
- terms and conditions relating to holiday entitlement, holiday pay and sickness pay
- length of notice required by either party
- disciplinary rules.

employer's obligations

In accordance with law, employers must observe certain obligations towards the people who work for them. They should:

- Pay their employees, so long as they are available for work. This means that even if employers have no work for their staff, they must still pay them. They cannot simply pick and choose the days on which there is work to do.
- Ensure that employees are safe while doing their jobs. Where special personal protective equipment is required, employers are required to provide it at their cost. Employees are not expected to pay for protective gear out of their own pockets.
- Refund employees for expenses incurred at or during work.
- Act in a reasonable manner towards their employees. They are obliged to do this under a duty of mutual trust and understanding, and this can be inferred or interpreted in many ways: actions such as harassment or demoting employees represent typical breaches of this duty. Such behaviour may enable employees to sue for damages for breach of contract. In more extreme situations, employees may be able to treat themselves as having been sacked without justification. This procedure is known as constructive dismissal.

employees' obligations

Employees are required, under a duty of good faith and loyalty, to:

- Devote their time during working hours to their employer's business. They may not use this time to pursue their own interests.
- Not reveal any confidential information relating to their employer's business to others.
- Disclose details of intellectual property to their employer; ownership of such designs, creations, discoveries or inventions derived at work, remain the property of the employer.
- Do their job diligently and properly; an employee who is grossly negligent may be dismissed without compensation or even be sued by their employer for any loss suffered as a result.
- Be honest within their employment; workers must not profit at their employer's expense.
- Obey reasonable instructions during their employment and carry out the job that they were employed to do.

national minimum wage

Statutory rules for minimum hourly rates first came into effect in April 1999. These now state that employees aged between 18 and 21 must receive at least £3.20 per hour. For employees over 21 years the minimum has been set at £3.70. (Note that tips paid directly to staff by customers do not contribute to the minimum hourly pay rate and are therefore not affected by this statute.)

national minimum wage and junior staff

There are exemptions to these rules which are applicable to those under training, i.e. under contracts of apprenticeship, or the government's modern apprenticeship scheme. A general overview is provided in the following table.

Age	Minimum wage	Considered as ...
16	none	exempt
17	none	exempt
18	£3.00 per hour	exemption 1
19–21	£3.00 per hour	exemption 2
22–25	£3.60 per hour	exemption 2 or 3
26 and over	£3.60 per hour	none apply

▲ minimum wage and training

exemption 1

If the trainees are under a contract of apprenticeship or taking part in the government's modern apprenticeship scheme, they are exempt from the minimum wage.

exemption 2

If the trainees are apprentices in their first year, they will be exempt from the minimum wage during that first year only.

exemption 3

If the trainees are apprentices in their first year, they will be exempt from the minimum wage during that first year only. But if they are doing accredited training with you and they are within the first six months of their employment, you must then pay them £3.20 per hour for that six-month period.

The above information was received from the DTI Minimum Wage Hotline; for more information contact the Department of Trade and Industry on 0845 6000 678.

working time regulations
48-hour working week

Under this current legislation no employee may work more than an average of 48 hours a week. This hourly average should be calculated over a 17-week period.

The regulations define work as 'Working at employer's disposal and carrying out his or her duties'. The table below helps to define some of the grey areas associated with what 'does' and 'does not' constitute work.

Being on call	Not work
Travelling to your job	Not work
At lunch	Not work
Driving as part of a job	Work
Working Breakfast or Lunch	Work
Taking work home (this refers to individuals taking work home of their own accord and not part of a working arrangement)	Not work

Employees can opt out of this law if they want to, but must:

- Have an agreement in writing signed by both parties
- Be allowed to bring the agreement to an end with appropriate notice.

Employers must:

- Keep a copy of the agreement stating the actual hours worked by the employee.

compulsory rest periods

A worker is entitled to a rest period of 11 consecutive hours between each working day. A worker is also entitled to an uninterrupted rest period of not less than 24 hours in each 7-day period. (This may be averaged out over 2 weeks, i.e. a worker is hence entitled to 2 days' consecutive rest within a fortnight.)

rest breaks at work

A worker is entitled to an uninterrupted break each working day. The break must be for at least 20 minutes. This cannot be taken at the beginning or the end of the working day.

adolescent workers

An adolescent worker is someone who is between school leaver age (usually 16) and under 18 years of age. They are given additional rights:

- Each day they must have at least 12 hours' uninterrupted rest in each 24-hour period
- Each week they must have 2 days' (48 hours') rest in each week (this can be reduced where it can be justified for technical or organisational reasons)
- The averaging of hours for weekly rest periods, applicable for adult workers, may not be used
- Adolescents are entitled to a rest period of 30 minutes when the working day is more than four and a half hours long.

holiday pay under the working time regulations

All employees, i.e. both full-time and part-time, are entitled to four weeks' holiday pay. This right applies only to employees who are employed continuously for more than 13 weeks. Holiday pay must be calculated at a rate equal to the averaged income over the previous 12 weeks, so therefore in situations where commissions are added to basic pay, this must be taken into consideration.

Note that there is no statutory entitlement to Bank or Public holidays.

statutory minimum notice

After one month of employment, employers and employees are required to give each other not less than one week's notice at any time.

After the completion of two years' employment, the employee is entitled to one week's notice for each year of employment, up to a maximum of 12 weeks' notice, whilst the employer maintains the right to only one week's notice.

statutory sick pay (SSP)

An employee is entitled to SSP after the completion of 3 months' continuous employment and adequate contributions in relation to National Insurance Contributions. In order to qualify, an employee must earn above the lower earnings limit (LEL).

The employee is not paid for the first three days of absence, but SSP of up to 28 weeks is then payable in any three-year period.

statutory maternity pay (SMP)

An employee is eligible to receive statutory maternity pay from her employer provided that she has been continuously employed for a period of 26 weeks by the 15th week (i.e. the **qualifying week**) before the expected week of confinement (**EWC** – also known as expected week of childbirth) and has received an average weekly wage at or above the LEL, i.e. £66.50 in 1999–2000. Working women earning less than this are not entitled to SMP but may be eligible to other benefits or financial assistance.

An employee cannot claim SMP prior to the 11th week before the EWC. After this, employees are entitled to and may receive SMP for an 18-week period. During the 18-week period, two rates of SMP are payable.

higher rate SMP

The higher rate is payable for the first 6 weeks. This is calculated at a rate of 90 per cent of normal earnings. When an employee is paid weekly, the calculations are made by averaging the employee's wage over the previous 8 weeks prior to the last pay day before the end of the **qualifying week**. When an employee is paid monthly, the weekly SMP rate is calculated by adding together the total pay received in the two months up to and including the last pay day prior to the end of the qualifying week, multiplying by 6 and dividing by 52.

lower rate SMP

The lower rate is payable for the remainder of the period, for up to 12 weeks. This is a flat rate of £59.55 in 1999–2000.

maternity rights

All employees' rights in relation to maternity are contained in the **Employment Rights Act 1996**, the **Sex Discrimination Act 1975** and the **Social Security Act 1986**. These provide employees with the following:

- The right to paid time off work for antenatal care
- The right to maternity leave and, where applicable, maternity absence
- The right to receive payment and benefits, if applicable, while absent because of pregnancy
- The right to return to work
- Protection from discrimination.

notifying the employer

An employee must inform her employer at least 21 days before she intends to start maternity leave, if she is to take advantage of SMP.

The employee must give her employer written notice:

- Of the fact that she is pregnant and confirmation of the expected week of childbirth (see Form MATB1)
- Of the date on which she expects to begin her maternity leave, which cannot be any earlier than the 11th week before EWC.

She will also need to provide a date to her employer on which she intends to start receiving SMP (no earlier than the 11th week before the EWC). And if she is eligible for maternity absence, she will need to provide written notice that she intends to return to work after this period. Note that the employee maintains the right to change her mind at some later time.

maternity leave and maternity absence

Maternity leave is available to all employees, regardless of how long they have worked for an employer, and is currently 18 weeks. The earliest time that employees can commence their leave is at the 11th week before the EWC; this date is confirmed in **Form MATB1** (this form is issued by their doctor around the 26th week of pregnacy and provides an expected week of childbirth EWC).

If a woman wishes to work beyond the 36th week of pregnancy, the employer can request written confirmation of her fitness to work. In order for the woman to maintain her statutory rights, the maternity leave must begin at the EWC or the birthdate if it is earlier. After childbirth, all employees are required by law to take a minimum 2 weeks' leave.

Maternity absence is an extended period, following on from leave for employees who satisfy certain requirements – they must have completed at least 1 year of continuous employment prior to the 11th EWC – and lasts for a period beyond normal maternity leave – up to 28 weeks after the week in which the child was born.

employees' rights on returning to work

Employees returning to work after **maternity leave** are entitled to return to exactly the same job on the same terms and conditions as prior to pregnancy.

Employees returning to work after **maternity absence** are also entitled to return to exactly the same job with the same terms and conditions. If this is no longer practicable, or the job role has become redundant, she must be offered suitable alternative employment within the organisation.

Employees' rights on returning to work after maternity leave or maternity absence are similar, except for one exclusion. **Small employers' rights**, i.e. where the employer has five or fewer staff, may not allow the employee to return to work after maternity absence.

recovery of SMP payments by employers

In most cases the payments made to employees in respect of SMP are recovered by the deduction of monies due to Inland Revenue in respect of PAYE and NICs. Employers can normally be reimbursed 92 per cent of the SMP paid out. However, for employers whose previous tax year's gross National Insurance Contributions amount to £20,000 or less, they can deduct the total amount due plus an additional 7 per cent.

employees' rights on the sale of a business

An employer may decide that he wants to sell up and in the past a business sale was sometimes an effective way of dumping the responsibility of the seller. The incoming buyer was absolved of any responsibility for the existing employees and often these people became redundant.

In 1981 the government, as a result of European laws, were required to interpret the Acquired Rights Directive (ARD). This led to the development of the **Transfer of Undertakings (Protection of Employment) Regulations 1981 (TUPE)**.

Now, employees have the TUPE regulations to protect employment following a business sale. However, these regulations are complex and there are several factors that must be considered. The main aspect that needs to be addressed relates to the business itself. Does the business for which the employee worked prior to sale, retain the same identity after the transfer to the new purchaser? For example:

- Were any assets transferred during the sale?
- Was the nature of the business carried on before the sale similar to that of the business after the sale?
- Was there any interruption of business activity?
- Were any employees taken on?

For the sale of a business which generally provides the relevant responses to these questions, the owner of the new business becomes the employer of the existing staff. This means that the new employer takes over the responsibility of the terms and conditions of employment for the employees.

transfer of employees in a business sale

Under the TUPE regulations the following conditions apply: only employees who are employed in the business immediately prior to the date of transfer will go to the new owner, and only the employees employed in the part of the business being sold will be transferred.

Employees transferring to the new ownership will enjoy the benefits of exactly the same terms and conditions as before. These include salary, fringe benefits, holiday entitlements etc. but there is one exception: the new employer does not have to replicate any terms in respect of an occupational pension scheme. (Useful information and further reading can be found in *Employment Rights on the Transfer of an Undertaking (PL699)*, from DTI Publications.)

■ termination of employment and employee rights

Employment may be brought to an end in a variety of different ways and may give rise to a claim for compensation. Termination of employment may be by:

- Notice
- Mutual agreement
- Expiry of fixed-term contract
- Breach of contract (employer's or employee's).

termination by notice

This is the most common route by which employment comes to an end; either the employee resigns or the employer dismisses the employee. The length of notice provided depends on the contract of employment. If a contract of employment does not exist then the **Employment Rights Act 1996** provides a statutory minimum to which both parties are subjected.

paying off an employee

Many contracts of employment contain a 'pay-in-lieu of notice' clause. This clause provides the employer with the right to pay off the employee within any notice period with a sum equal to their salary value. Thus an alternative method exists to terminate employment, other than requiring the person to work out their notice.

resignation by an employee

When a resignation is received, the termination of employment takes effect immediately; it can only be withdrawn with the employer's consent. If the employee leaves before the end of the notice period, the employee is in breach of contract and the employer may sue for damages.

dismissal by the employer

When dismissal of an employee occurs, attention must be given to the employee's contractual and statutory rights (see below).

termination by mutual agreement

This type of termination can occur automatically in certain pre-determined situations, for example after a takeover or relocation of business.

fixed-term contracts

A fixed-term contract will state from the outset the pre-determined length of employment, which may be relatively short, say 3 months, or long term. This type of contract will clearly state a commencement date and expiration date.

termination by breach
employee's breach

There are certain situations where the employer is entitled to terminate the contract of employment of an employee immediately. These may be:

- gross misconduct or gross negligence
- conviction for criminal offence
- persistent breaches of the contract
- conduct considered to bring the employee or employer into disrepute
- unauthorised disclosure of confidential information.

Normally, the more serious the breach, the more likely it is to justify dismissal without notice. Likewise, dismissal may be the result of a number of minor incidents concluding with one minor breach that proves to be the final straw.

gross misconduct and gross negligence

Acts of gross misconduct can be assumed in any of the following situations: theft, drug abuse, racial or sexual harassment, drunkeness or assault. On the other hand, gross negligence could be presumed in a situation where an employee has totally ignored safety procedure which has resulted in a serious accident.

employer's breach

The most common breach of contract committed by employers is the failure to provide sufficient notice of dismissal, and may lead to the following consequences:

- a claim for damages for wrongful dismissal
- a potential claim of unfair dismissal
- the invalidation of restrictive clauses within the contract of employment.

constructive dismissal

Constructive dismissal occurs when an employee treats themselves as having been dismissed as the result of the employer committing a serious breach of contract. Behaviour that would typically justify an employee in considering themselves constructively dismissed may include: significant pay cut, demotion, humiliating the employee in front of other employees, suspension without pay, false accusations, and racial or sexual harassment.

employees' rights on termination of employment

Employees who have been dismissed without compensation will pursue their rights and will investigate ways in which they can enforce them. These rights fall into two categories: contractual claims and statutory claims.

In situations of **contractual claims**, dismissals in breach of contract are known as 'wrongful' or 'unlawful', whereas, in a **statutory claim**, dismissals in breach of statute (Employment Rights Act 1996) are known as 'unfair'.

Hence, if an employee is dismissed without due notice or justifiable reason, the contract will have been breached and the employee will have a potential claim for wrongful dismissal. Conversely, under present law, had this person received the correct period of notice and worked that period out in full, although no claim may be valid in respect of wrongful dismissal, the employee may have a potential claim for unfair dismissal, provided there has been one year's continuous employment.

fair dismissal

A dismissal would be considered fair if the employer can show that it was owing to one of the following reasons:

- misconduct
- lack of capability or qualification to do the job
- redundancy.

Misconduct can be demonstrated in a variety of different ways. In addition to acts of gross misconduct (see page 101) an employee may have been persistently late, refused to obey orders, taken unauthorised leave or used offensive language or behaviour.

Lack of capability would be assumed when an employee is incompetent. This could occur after a period of training and assessment, where the employee fails to achieve the expected appropriate standards of work.

Redundancy occurs when an employer requires fewer staff to do the work, and this could be due to a variety of reasons that result in business downturn.

fair dismissal procedure for misconduct

In any situation leading up to the dismissal of an employee for misconduct, an employer will need to show that a fair system had been adopted: firstly to establish the employee's guilt and secondly to execute the dismissal.

Employers with more than 20 employees are required by law to provide these employees with written details of the organisation's disciplinary procedure within their Statement of Particulars. Guidelines for these procedures can be obtained from the Advisory Conciliation and Arbitration Service (ACAS).

disciplinary hearing

In order for an employee to receive a fair hearing, a number of important measures should be taken:

1. An employee should receive, in good time, full details of any allegations made against him or her. The reference to 'in good time' will deter employers from bringing a disciplinary hearing without fair warning.
2. The employee should be given full access to all relevant information in order to defend him or herself properly. In situations where evidence from witnesses is to be used, the employee should have full access to cross-examine statements made against him or her. Similarly, an employee may elect to have the support of another work associate or trade union member/representation.
3. An employee should normally be given the right of appeal against any decision made against them.

fair procedure and dismissal for capability

In situations leading up to dismissal for lack of capability, the employer should consider the following factors:

1. Was the employee given sufficient training?
2. Did the employee receive warnings about sub-standard performance?
3. If targets were set, were they reasonable in the circumstances?
4. Would others have been dismissed in similar situations?

This may seem fairly clear cut if these factors were applied to the expected performance of, say, a senior stylist, but may not be so apparent in respect of a receptionist.

Other useful information relating to this subject can be found in *Fair and Unfair Dismissal: A Guide for Employers* (PL714), from DTI Publications.

■ personal development and measuring effectiveness

At work, managers of people use performance appraisal or progress reviews to evaluate the effectiveness of their team. An appraisal is a system, normally taking the form of an interview situation, in which you and your employee review and evaluate their personal contribution and/or progress over a predetermined period of time, as measured against expected targets or standards.

In personal development situations, a similar process would take place at suitable points within a personal programme of training in order to review progress and training effectiveness, measured against specific training objectives.

To measure progress towards training targets as well as overall work contributions, there needs to be clear stated expectations of the performance required. For both training and work activities, this is the standard to which competence will need to be demonstrated.

In training situations, trainees undergo a programme of training which states:

■ what training activities will take place
■ what tasks need to be performed
■ what standards are expected to be reached
■ when assessment should be expected
■ when a review of progress towards the agreed targets is to take place.

However, in normal ongoing work situations, performance appraisal will be based on the following factors:

■ results achieved against set objectives and job requirements
■ any additional accomplishments and contributions
■ contributions made by the individual as compared with those of other staff members.

The job requirements would be outlined in the employee's job description (see pages 83–84). A job description is a written specification of the main purposes and functions expected within a given job. Good job descriptions will include details of the following:

■ the job title
■ the work location(s)
■ responsibility (to whom, and for what)
■ the job purpose
■ main functions (listed)
■ standards expected
■ any special conditions.

Standards expected from the job holder will often include standards of behaviour and appearance. If these have been stated from the outset, the job holder will know exactly what is expected of them.

the appraisal process

At the beginning of the appraisal period, the manager and the employee jointly discuss, develop, and mutually agree the objectives and performance measures for that period. An action plan will then be drafted, outlining the expected outcomes.

During the appraisal period, should there be any significant changes in factors such as objectives or performance measures, these will be discussed between the manager and employee and any amendments will be appended to the action plan.

At the end of the appraisal period, the results are discussed by the employee and the manager, and both manager and employee sign the appraisal. A copy is prepared for the employee and the original is kept on file.

An appraisal of performance will contain the following information:

■ employee's name
■ appraisal period
■ appraiser's name and title
■ performance objectives
■ job title
■ work location
■ results achieved
■ identified areas of strength and weakness, with ongoing action plan
■ overall performance grading (optional).

Performance Appraisal

Name:	Jane Manners
Job Title:	Trainee stylist
Date of Appraisal:	28 April 2000
Objectives:	To obtain competence within: Cutting hair – layering techniques across the ranges Blow-drying hair – on a variety of hair types and lengths.
Notes of Achievement:	– competence has been achieved across the range for all the cutting requirements. – competence has been achieved for most blow drying range requirements
Training Requirements:	Further training and practice is needed within the areas of blow drying longer length effects.
Any other comments on performance by Appraiser:	Jane has achieved most of the objectives set out during the last appraisal.
Any comments on the Appraisal by the staff Appraised:	I feel that this has been a fair appraisal of my progress although I did not achieve all of my performance targets. Jane Manners
Action Plan:	– To achieve occupational competence across the range for blow drying (i.e. longer hair length hair). – To undergo training and practice in perming methods and techniques. – To take assessment for perming.
Date of Next Appraisal:	27 October 2000

self-appraisal

In order for you to manage yourself within the job role, you need to encourage staff to carry out self-appraisal. Help them to identify for themselves the expectations of the job and also the areas where there is room for improvement. Measuring their own strengths and weaknesses against laid-down performance criteria (as found in the NVQ Level 3 standards of competence) is one way of monitoring their own progress. They would simply use the performance criteria set out within the standards as a checklist, and this will help them to:

- identify areas where further training is required
- identify areas where further practice is required
- identify areas where competence can be achieved.

the chain of delegation: the supervisor

Managers are the people who make decisions about the running of the business. Often they are administrators who lack the technical expertise to assess or evaluate the individual performances of stylists and trainees. It is the supervisor, therefore, who bridges the gap between strategic planning and shop-floor activities: the supervisor is the key link in communication.

The salon supervisor will assist you in allocating work to the staff. Since the supervisor also reports back on the effectiveness and efficiency of individual and team performances, this individual must be able to analyse and evaluate working practices, and when necessary must make spontaneous decisions about staff cover in the event of abnormal working conditions. Systematic allocation of tasks and contingency planning by the supervisor ensure the smooth, efficient operation of the business.

the supervisor's role

Strategic planning is the manager's responsibility, however it is the job of the supervisor to support you in your decisions.

The supervisor will be directly involved with the implementation of practices and procedures, and because of this technical expertise, should be able to monitor progress and evaluate the effectiveness of any plan. If systems are found to be unworkable, the supervisor should be able to help by recommending alternative solutions or courses of action.

Whenever you change a plan or system, the change has some effect on someone or something. Your supervisor may be better placed than you to foresee the implications of a proposed change. A supervisor giving feedback based on informed opinion is supportive in a positive way, not a threat.

A supervisor would be expected to have a working knowledge of the legislation and the company policy that affect the working environment. Some recommendations for change, although sound in principle, may not be possible to put into practice because of legal constraints. In these situations, alternative solutions must then be sought.

the supervisor supporting staff

The required level of support given during training will mean that your supervisor should be able to coach individuals while they learn. Supervisory support can be quite different from training support. You are concerned with the overall effectiveness and the efficiency of the tasks being performed, whereas your supervisor will be supporting you and the staff by casually observing on a day-to-day basis, and perhaps providing feedback as and when necessary. In situations where issues need to be addressed promptly, you would expect matters to be dealt with tactfully but firmly. This is especially important when it is evident that an employee:

- is putting others at risk
- is not yet competent in a given activity
- needs further instruction or training.

problems with individuals

A particular member of staff may show evidence of an 'attitude problem' or unacceptable behaviour. In doing so, this individual may upset other members of staff, or even your clients. It is essential that you select an appropriate time and a private place to discuss this with the individual, explaining the problem as you see

it and listening to the other person's point of view. You must show a caring but firm attitude when dealing with disruptive behaviour: failure to do so may make the situation worse. In particular, if you don't listen as well as talk, you may push this member of staff into being rebellious and uncooperative. Remember, any judgements you make should be based on facts and informed opinion, not supposition and rumour.

Information of a personal or private nature must always be handled with discretion.

equal opportunities

In the past, staff in many organisations felt that they were at a disadvantage because of their sex, race or disability. Changing attitudes and the easing of European trade restrictions have improved this situation, but you need to be vigilant in preventing any discrimination.

Employment legislation (see Appendix 1) now requires codes of practice and policy statements which address these issues: these should be provided by all companies. The following is an example of an equal opportunities statement, produced by the Department of Employment.

> **EQUAL OPPORTUNITIES STATEMENT**
>
> The company wholeheartedly supports the principle of equal opportunities in employment and opposes all forms of unlawful or unfair discrimination on the grounds of colour, race, nationality, ethnic or national origin, sex, being married or disability. We believe that it is in the company's best interests, and those of all who work in it, to ensure that the human resources, talents and skills available throughout the community are considered when employment opportunities arise.
>
> To this end, within the framework of the law, we are committed, wherever practicable, to achieving and maintaining a workforce which broadly reflects the local community in which we operate.
>
> Every possible step will be taken to ensure that individuals are treated equally and fairly and that decisions on recruitment, selection, training, promotion and career management are based solely on objective and job-related criteria.

disciplinary action

Your company will have standards and expectations relating to conduct and behaviour. Preventative action is better than cure, so staff will be happier in their work if they know what is expected of them. These rules and working conditions can be clarified and displayed through job descriptions and organisational policy.

organisational policy

Within an organisation's policy there should be an outline of the required performance levels relating to each aspect of the business:

■ health and safety procedures
■ security of company resources systems and documentation
■ staff relationships
■ customer care and company goodwill
■ punctuality and absence
■ dismissible offences (usually forms of gross misconduct)
■ grievance procedures.

The organisational policy should be displayed or individually copied to all concerned. Many companies produce a handbook or guide (mandatory if you employ more than 20 people) which is given to new staff members during their induction. This may contain policy statements as well as legal requirements.

disciplinary action: a suggested procedure

If staff members fail to meet the required standards, they should expect disciplinary action to be taken against them.

It is wise to have a formal procedure for this, with known stages:

Stage 1.   Verbal warning. This should be witnessed, and the date and circumstances recorded in case it is necessary to refer to it later.

Stage 2.   Second verbal warning. Again, this should be witnessed and documented. Note that it must concern the same matter as the first warning.

Stage 3.   Final (written) warning. This must be given to the staff member in writing. It should refer to the previous verbal warnings. A final warning could result in dismissal, so only the manager can implement this action.

Stage 4.   Dismissal.

If disciplinary action results in a third and final warning, the manager will conduct an interview with the employee in order to:

■ establish the facts
■ weigh the evidence
■ decide the future course of action.

Your supervisor may be involved either in gathering evidence or in presenting it at the interview.

The Advisory Conciliation and Arbitration Service (ACAS) has produced the following guidelines governing dismissal:

DISCIPLINARY PROCEDURE
(guidelines provided by ACAS)

All actions should:

1. Be in writing.

2. Specify to whom it applies.

3. Provide for matters to be dealt with quickly.

4. Indicate the disciplinary action that may be taken.

5. Specify the levels of management which have authority to take various forms of disciplinary action, ensuring that immediate superiors do not formally have the powers to dismiss without reference to senior management.

6. Provide for all individuals to be informed of the complaints against them and to be given the opportunity to state their case before decisions are reached.

7. Give individuals the right to be accompanied by a trade union representative or fellow employee of their choice.

8. Ensure that, except for gross misconduct, no employees are dismissed for a first breach of discipline.

9. Ensure that disciplinary action is not taken until the case has been carefully investigated.

10. Ensure that individuals are given an explanation for any penalties imposed.

11. Provide a right of appeal and specify the procedure to be followed.

grievance procedure

Employees should have a clear route to pursue grievance procedures, and this route should be stated within the organisational policy. The nature of the grievance is incidental: employees should be encouraged – and given every opportunity – to state their particular grievance to the management:

The grievance procedure should clearly indicate:

- that it exists to resolve disputes quickly
- who should be contacted
- what form of evidence is required
- that matters are dealt with confidentially
- that representation is available, and what form this takes.

■ paying wages and PAYE
summary

Paying your employees' wages may be carried out on either a weekly or monthly basis. Depending on which pay interval you choose, you will need to calculate the salary payable, including any commissions, bonuses, overtime etc. (i.e. the gross amount) less the necessary deductions made from wages in respect of Income Tax and National Insurance Contributions (i.e. the nett amount). These amounts, including your own Employer's National Insurance Contributions, will be paid to the Collector of Taxes by your organisation on a monthly or quarterly basis. Accurate records relating to PAYE must be kept for six years and made available (on request) to Inland Revenue and the Contributions Agency.

technical talk

PAYE	Pay As You Earn, a system for deducting Income Tax at source
NICs	National Insurance Contributions
P45	A document relating to an employee, showing Tax Code, National Insurance number and other personal data
P11	Deductions Working Sheet – completed for each employee and showing details of salary paid and deductions made
Pay Adjustment Tables	A system for working out free-of-tax pay to date for employees
Taxable Pay Tables	Used in conjunction with Pay Adjustment Tables to work out the tax due from taxable pay
N.I. Tables	A system for calculating the NIC deduction from an employee's gross salary as well as the Employer's NIC in respect of their employee
Tax Code	A code issued by Inland Revenue for an employee which is used to calculate tax deductions
P14	An End-Of-Year Summary used for each employee on which to record the totals from form P11
P35	An Employer's Annual Return showing details of all employees' PAYE and NICs collectively

PAYE and NICs: the legal requirements

During the tax year you must:

- ✓ deduct the correct amount of PAYE from your employees' pay
- ✓ work out how much NICs you (as employer) and your employees have to pay
- ✓ keep accurate records of your employees' pay and PAYE and NICs due
- ✓ make monthly (or quarterly) payments of the total PAYE and NICs due to Inland Revenue.

At the end of the tax year you must:

- ✓ send a return to the Tax Office showing details of each employee's total pay and the PAYE and NICs due (P14)
- ✓ send details to the Tax Office about certain expenses you have paid to employees, or benefits you have provided them
- ✓ provide each employee who has paid PAYE and NICs with a P60 showing their pay PAYE and NIC details
- ✓ give your employees a copy of the information you have given to the Tax Office relating to their expenses or benefits.

working out the wages
what do I need?
(Current versions of)

- ✓ Pay Adjustment Tables
- ✓ Taxable Pay Tables
- ✓ National Insurance Tables
- ✓ Form P11 - a Deductions Working Sheet
- ✓ Employee's Tax Code.

PAYE codes

Your employees are issued with a tax code, which you will receive from the tax office. The number portion of the code, such as **182L**, denotes the tax allowances which are due against the employee's pay. Each code number is followed by a letter, such as 182**L**, and this suffix code indicates the type of personal allowances given in the code. The letters A, H, J, L, P, T, V and Y all indicate something different. For example, the letter H includes married couples allowance.

A code starting with the letter D, i.e. a D code, means that all of the employee's pay should be taxed at the higher rate. Similarly, a code starting with BR means that tax is to be deducted at the basic rate.

income tax rates

The percentage of tax in the £, i.e. the taxation rate, will vary from time to time, but currently there are three tax rates:

Starter Rate of 10 per cent on earnings up to £1,500

Basic Rate of 23 per cent on earnings between £1,501 and £28,000

Higher Rate of 40 per cent on earnings over £28,000

So, depending on each employee's earnings, you will be using one of three Tax Tables, i.e. SR, B, C&D. See the example that follows.

pay adjustment tables

The pay adjustment tables can be used for either weekly or monthly payment cycles. These tables are used to help you to calculate the amount of free pay (pay free of tax) for your employees in any week or month relative to their tax code.

1. Turn to the appropriate page in Table A corresponding to the pay date and the pay cycle, for example **Week 1**, **Week 2**, **Week 3** etc. or **Month 1**, **Month 2** etc.

2. In the column headed 'Code' find the number which corresponds to the employee's Tax Code (for calculation purposes, you may ignore any suffix letters, such as L in 182L). The amount of free pay to date is shown to the right of the code. See the extract from Table A on page 109.

In the extract, we see that for code 182L for month 6, the free-of-tax pay is £914.52.

taxable pay tables

The taxable pay tables show you how much to deduct from the wages in respect of an employee's tax. For employees with Code BR you would automatically use the basic rate tax tables, Table B. For those with Code D you would always use the higher rate tables, Table D.

For employees with other codes you would use a quick look-up chart to see which taxable pay table you should use.

Using the extract shown on lower part of page 109, we look at the month number, which then indicates the highest amount for which each table can be used. Looking across the columns from 1 to 2, when you find an amount that is the same or more than the employee's total taxable pay, you use the table shown under this heading. If the employee's total taxable pay is more than column 2, then Tables C&D are used.

Month 6
Sept 6 to Oct 5

TABLE A - PA\`

Code	Total pay adjustment to date £	Code	Total pay adjustment to date £	Code	Total pay adjustment to date £	Code	Total pay adjustment to date £	Code	Total pay adjustment to date £
0	NIL								
1	9.54	61	309.54	121	609.54	181	909.54	241	1209.54
2	14.52	62	314.52	122	614.52	182	914.52	242	1214.52
3	19.50	63	319.50	123	619.50	183	919.50	243	1219.50
4	24.54	64	324.54	124	624.54	184	924.54	244	1224.54
5	29.52	65	329.52	125	629.52	185	929.52	245	1229.52
6	34.50	66	334.50	126	634.50	186	934.50	246	1234.50
7	39.54	67	339.54	127	639.54	187	939.54	247	1239.54

▲ extract from Table A

Month	Column 1 Use Table SR on page 5 £	Column 2 Use Tables B on pages 8 & 9 £
1	125	2334
2	250	4667
3	375	7000
4	500	9334
5	625	11667
6	750	14000
7	875	16334
8	1000	18667
9	1125	21000
10	1250	23334
11	1375	25667
12	1500	28000

▲ which table do I use? (extract from taxable pay tables, May 1999 issue)

which table do I use?
example 1

By looking at the two extracts from the tables shown above, we can work out which table to use. Let's say that you have an employee with a Tax Code **242L** and the payment is made in **Month 6**:

Pay for the month	£305
The previous pay to date is	£1,525.00
Total pay to date is 305 + 1525 =	£1,830.00
Now deducting their free pay for **Month 6 Table A**	£1,214.52 from the total pay, we arrive at
Total taxable pay to date	**£615.48**

We can now see that the total taxable pay to date **does not exceed £750** (see extract on lower part of page 109), so we would use **Table SR** for this particular employee.

example 2

We now have an employee with a Tax Code **185L** and payment to be made in **Month 6**:

Pay for the month	£1,050
The previous pay to date is	£5,250.00
Total pay to date is 1050 + 5250 =	£6,300.00
Now deducting their free pay for **Month 6**	£929.52 from the total pay we arrive at
Total taxable pay to date	**£5,370.48**

In this situation we see that this figure exceeds the **Table SR** (col. 1) figure for **Month 6** (£750) but **does not exceed £14,000** (in col. 2). So therefore in this case **Table B** will be used.

how do I calculate the right amount of tax to deduct?

Using the information in **Example 1**, we have an employee with a Tax Code **242L** to be paid in **Month 6**:

Pay for the month	£305
The previous pay to date is	£1,525.00
Total pay to date is 305 + 1525 =	£1,830.00
Now deducting their free pay for **Month 6 Table A**	£1,214.52 from the total pay we arrive at
Total taxable pay to date	**£615.48**

We can now see that the total taxable pay to date **does not exceed £750** (see extract on lower part of page 109), so we would use **Table SR** for this particular employee.

We now need to calculate the amount of tax to deduct from the total taxable pay. We turn to **Table SR** (see extract in right-hand column of this page).

Looking down the table to find the tax payable on £615.48 first of all, we need to round down the figure to a whole number of pounds (£615). Now, taking the figure £600, look in the corresponding column, i.e. £60.00. We now take the figure £15 and find that the tax due is £1.50. By adding these together we arrive at

Total tax payable to date for **Month 6** is £60 + £1.50 = £61.50 (the 10 per cent Starter Rate)

We can accept that tax would have been deducted in previous months, so a simple subtraction of the total tax deducted in Month 5 will be deducted from this figure in order to show tax payable for Month 6. This accumulative system of calculation is shown below in the extract from the Deductions Working Sheet for Example 2, on page 113.

Pages 2 and 3 tell you when to use this table

Where the exact amount of taxable pay is not shown, add together the figures for two (or more) entries to make up the amount of taxable pay to the nearest £1 below.

Tax Due on Taxable Pay from £100 to £1500		Tax Due on Taxable Pay from £1 to £99			
Total TAXABLE PAY to date	Total TAX DUE to date	Total TAXABLE PAY to date	Total TAX DUE to date	Total TAXABLE PAY to date	Total TAX DUE to date
£	£	£	£	£	£
100	10.00	1	0.10	50	5.00
200	20.00	2	0.20	51	5.10
300	30.00	3	0.30	52	5.20
400	40.00	4	0.40	53	5.30
500	50.00	5	0.50	54	5.40
600	60.00	6	0.60	55	5.50
700	70.00	7	0.70	56	5.60
800	80.00	8	0.80	57	5.70
900	90.00	9	0.90	58	5.80
1000	100.00	10	1.00	59	5.90
1100	110.00	11	1.10	60	6.00
1200	120.00	12	1.20	61	6.10
1300	130.00	13	1.30	62	6.20
1400	140.00	14	1.40	63	6.30
1500	150.00	15	1.50	64	6.40
		16	1.60	65	6.50

Inland Revenue

▲ extract from Table SR

Using the information in **Example 2**, we have an employee with a Tax Code **185L** to be paid in **Month 6**:

Pay for the month	£1,050
The previous pay to date is	£5,250.00
Total pay to date is 1050 + 5250 =	£6,300.00
Now deducting their free pay for **Month 6**	£929.52 from the total pay we arrive at
Total taxable pay to date	**£5,370.48**

We now need to calculate the amount of tax to deduct from the total taxable pay. Using **Table B** (see extract below) to work out tax at 23 per cent, we shall also be making a subtraction from the amount to give the benefit of the Starter Rate relief at the lower tax rate of 10 per cent.

Looking down the table to find the tax payable on £5,370.48 we will firstly round down the figure to a whole number of pounds (£5,370). Now taking the figure £5,300, look in the corresponding column, i.e. £1219. We now take the figure £70 and find that the tax due is £16.10. By adding these together we arrive at £1219 + £16.10 = £1,235.10. We now look in the subtraction table to find the starting rate relief for month 6, i.e. £97.50. Therefore

Total tax payable to date for **Month 6** is £1,235.10 − £97.50 = **£1,137.60**

Again, we can accept that tax would have been deducted in previous months, so a simple subtraction of month 5 from month 6 will show the amount of tax payable in month 6 (see the extract from the Deductions Working Sheet on page 113).

Table B Tax at 23%

From £100 to £27,100		From £1 to £99		Subtraction Table to give Starting rate rate relief 10%	
Total Taxable Pay to date	Total Tax Due to date	Total Taxable Pay to date	Total Tax Due to date	Month no.	Amount to subtract £
				1	16.25
4,900	1,127	66	15.18	2	32.50
5,000	1,150	67	15.41	3	48.75
5,100	1,173	68	15.64	4	65.00
5,200	1,196	69	15.87	5	81.25
5,300	1,219	70	16.10	6	97.50
5,400	1,242	71	16.33	7	113.75

how do I calculate the right amount of National Insurance to deduct?

The Contributions Agency provide employers with tables for the purpose of calculatiing National Insurance Contributions. These tables clearly show how much the employee and employer must pay on either weekly or monthly intervals.

There are three different sets of tables for Not-Contracted-Out contributions:

Table A For male employees aged 16 to 64 or female employees aged 16 to 59 or any employee with appropriate personal pension.

Table B For married women or widows aged under 60 who are entitled to pay employee's contributions at the reduced rate.

Table C For men and women beyond normal retirement age.

Using the information from **Example 1**, we have an employee aged 16 whose pay for the month was £305 and from **Example 2**, we have an employee aged 25 whose pay for the month was £1,050. We can now calculate their respective National Insurance Contributions (see extracts from tables on page 112). Note that where the exact gross pay is not shown in the table, the next smaller figure is used.

Employee's Earnings up to and including the UEL	Earnings at the LEL (Where earnings reach or exceed the LEL) 1a	Earnings above the LEL, up to and including the *employee's* Earnings Threshold 1b	Earnings above the *employee's* Earnings Threshold, up to and including the *employer's* Earnings Threshold 1c	Earnings above the *employer's* Earnings Threshold, up to and including the UEL 1d	Total of employee's and employer's contributions payable 1e	Employee's contributions payable 1f	Employer's contributions
£	£	£	£	£	£ P	£ P	£ P
Up to and including 290.99	No NIC Liability, make no entries on forms P11 and P14						
291	291	0	0	0	0.00	0.00	0.00
295	291	4	0	0	0.00	0.00	0.00
299	291	8	0	0	0.00	0.00	0.00
303	291	12	0	0	0.00	0.00	0.00
307	291	16	0	0	0.00	0.00	0.00
311	291	20	0	0	0.00	0.00	0.00
1023	291	38	36	658	150.12	69.60	80.52
1027	291	38	36	662	151.01	70.00	81.01
1031	291	38	36	666	151.90	70.40	81.50
1035	291	38	36	670	152.78	70.80	81.98
1039	291	38	36	674	153.67	71.20	82.47
1043	291	38	36	678	154.56	71.60	82.96
1047	291	38	36	682	155.45	72.00	83.45
1051	291	38	36	686	156.34	72.40	83.94
1055	291	38	36	690	157.22	72.80	84.42
1059	291	38	36	694	158.11	73.20	84.91
1063	291	38	36	698	159.00	73.60	85.40
1067	291	38	36	702	159.89	74.00	85.89
1071	291	38	36	706	160.78	74.40	86.38
1075	291	38	36	710	161.66	74.80	86.86
1079	291	38	36	714	162.55	75.20	87.35

▲ extracts from not-contracted-out contributions for employers (monthly Table A)

Inland Revenue

In **Example 1**, an employee earning £305 will pay £1.80 National Insurance Contribution and their employer will pay nothing.

In a similar way, in **Example 2**, an employee earning £1,050 will pay £76.60 National Insurance Contribution and their employer will pay £84.30.

completing form P11 (deductions working sheet)

In this section we have explained how to calculate the deductions from employees' wages in respect of Tax and National Insurance and employer's NIC. This information must be accurately recorded for accounting and inspection purposes on Form P11 (Deductions Working Sheet).

A form P11 is maintained for each employee, see the example Form P11 on page 113.

From the completed form P11, you can now see how the cumulative totals of monthly salaries and deductions are recorded before individual pay packets are produced.

A completed P11 Deductions Working Sheet showing the section for National Insurance Contributions etc. (on the reverse side) is given on page 114.

Deductions Working Sheet P11   Year to 5 April 2000

Employee's details *in CAPITALS*

Box A Employer's name

Box B Tax Office and Reference

Box C Surname

Box D First two forenames

Box E National insurance no.

Box F Date of birth *in figures* — Day Month Year

Box G Works no. etc

For guidance on PAYE Income Tax and the completion of columns 2 to 8, see CWG1 'Employer's Quick Guide to PAYE and National Insurance Contributions'
- Card 8 for examples using suffix codes
- Card 9 for general completion
- Card 10 specifically for K codes, including examples.

† If amended cross out previous code.

Box J Tax code †

Box K Amended code †

Wk/Mth in which applied

Please keep this form for at least 3 years after the end of the year to which it relates, or longer if you are asked to do so.

Turn over page f...

PAYE Income Tax

Month no	Week no	Pay in the week or month including Statutory Sick Pay/ Statutory Maternity Pay 2 £ p	Total pay to date 3 £ p	Total free pay to date 4a £ p	K codes only — Total 'additional pay' to date (Table A) 4b £ p	Total taxable pay to date i.e. column 3 minus column 4a or column 3 plus column 4b 5 £ p	Total tax due to date as shown by Taxable Pay Tables 6 £ p	K codes only — Tax due at end of current period Mark refunds 'R' 6a £ p	Regulatory limit i.e. 50% of column 2 entry 6b £ p	Tax deducted or refunded in the week or month Mark refunds 'R' 7 £ p	K codes only — Tax not deducted owing to the Regulatory limit 8 £ p	For employer's use
	1											
	2											
	3											
1	4	1050 00	1050 00	154 92		895 08	189 60			189 60		
	5											
	6											
	7											
2	8	1050 00	2100 00	309 84		1790 16	379 20			189 60		
	9											
	10											
	11											
	12	1050 00	3150 00	464 76		2685 24	568 80			189 60		
3	13											
	14											
	15											
	16	1050 00	4200 00	619 68		3580 32	758 40			189 60		
4	17											
	18											
	19											
	20	1050 00	5250 00	774 60		4475 40	948 00			189 60		
5	21											
	22											
	23											
	24											
	25	1050 00	6300	929 52		5370 48	1137 60			189 60		
6	26											
	27											
	28											
	29											
7	30											
	31											
	32											

Inland Revenue

▲ completed form 11 deductions working sheet for employee of example 2

wages book and payments to employees

This section has helped to explain what is required in respect of using tables and recording the information for individual employees. For accounting purposes this information must also be recorded in a wages book. This will provide a single system for identifying all employees' PAYE and NICs for any single week/month throughout the year, at a glance. Wages/Salaries books may be purchased from any stationers or office supplier.

The entries made within the wages book will be copied directly from the relevant employee Form P11s and will show cumulative totals including all company/firm expenses in respect of salaries.

▲ reverse side of the completed P11 deductions working sheet, showing the section for national insurance contributions

payments

You may choose to pay your staff in cash, by cheque or by direct transfer into their bank account. Whichever method you choose will depend on your own company's/firm's policy, but you must provide your staff with an itemised pay statement. This statement must detail the following information:

- the gross wage
- the amount and purpose of any fixed deductions, such as trade union subscriptions, charitable donations, AVCs (additional voluntary contributions to personal pensions), health care etc.
- the amount and purpose of any variable deductions, such as PAYE and NICs
- The nett wage.

devising a pay formula

Setting up a reasonable salary scheme is a very difficult task, because the scheme will depend upon a number of business aspects. The business on the one hand will want to increase profitability, but on the other it should remain sensitive and responsive to business trends, client requests, staffing levels and the cost of sales. This trading balance is a critical factor.

In any salon situation, the main expectation of your stylists will be a fair reward for their work efforts. This reward will be money, primarily. The ability to earn more in the future will be the key motivational factor that will stimulate your staff. Other incentives from time to time may also reward achievement, and these may be in the form of: time off, recreational activities, promotional gifts and training.

The payment scheme options are:

- Flat rate
- Flat rate plus commission
- Variable rate plus commission.

flat rate

Paying your staff a flat (fixed) rate would be the simplest option, since you know in advance what your salary costs will be over the trading year, and the process eliminates difficult arithmetic and makes cash flow forecasting easier. However, this option neither recognises the individual's ability to achieve targets nor provides any ongoing stimulation or motivation.

flat rate plus commission

Paying your staff a fixed rate plus commission has, historically, been the popular option adopted by employers. This system rewards staff for their levels of achievement, but is more difficult to forecast over the trading year and may leave the business vulnerable in times of poor trading.

Variable rate plus commission

Paying your staff a variable rate plus commission provides an alternative to the above. This system of performance-related pay is now becoming a more popular option for those salons that have the technology to support it. If we take the principle that a salon's growth occurs by providing services and treatments to satisfied clients at a profit, we can then pass this rationale on to our staff.

Each stylist attracts a following of clients (client database). This number of satisfied clients will generate an income to the salon over a period of time, depending upon how soon they revisit, what services or treatments they receive and any new referrals they make.

So, by taking this rationale we can expect regular clients to come back within a set time-frame, and we can encourage occasional clients to come back more frequently (i.e. to become regulars). Therefore staff will be remunerated in two ways:

1. by a variable basic rate that is directly linked to the number of **active** clients within their client database, i.e. a rate reviewed monthly based on the clients that return within a fixed time-frame, and

2. by a variable commission related to the variable basic rate dependent on the income generated for the salon.

where do I get more information?
All of the forms and supporting information mentioned within this section are available to employers from Inland Revenue and the Contributions Agency. See Appendix 2.

employer's annual pack order line
0345 646646
This pack also contains *Employer's Quick Guide to PAYE and NICs* (Information pack CWG1), which will include useful information for completion of

- end-of-year returns
- end-of-year summaries (P14)
- statutory sick pay
- statutory maternity pay

health and safety at work
the law
The Health and Safety at Work Act 1974 (HASAW Act) is an act which has been dramatically transformed in recent years. It originally added to and partly replaced older health and safety at work legislation, such as the Factories Act 1961 and the Offices, Shops and Railway Premises Act 1963, and more recently incorporated health and safety legislation that complies with European directives.

The HASAW Act extended the scope of legislation, bringing all people at work within its range. Employers must comply with both the general duties contained in the HASAW Act as well as more specific requirements contained in earlier acts and/or subsequent regulations made under the HASAW Act. Health and Safety legislation is enforced by inspectors employed by the Health and Safety Executive and by local authorities. Inspectors have powers of access to premises, exceeding those of the police, should they have reason to believe that the law is being broken.

what the law requires
Under the Health and Safety at Work Act, you have to ensure the safety of yourself and others who may be affected by what you do. The term 'others' refers to

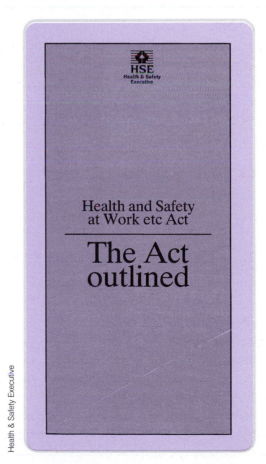

Health & Safety Executive

HEALTH & SAFETY POLICY

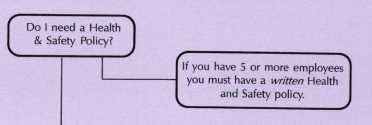

Do I need a Health & Safety Policy?

If you have 5 or more employees you must have a *written* Health and Safety policy.

HEALTH AND SAFETY POLICY GUIDANCE NOTES

1. Why have a Health and Safety policy?

An explicit Health and Safety policy demonstrates to your employees that you care for their health, safety and welfare. Writing the policy will help you to think through all the arrangements you have made or need to make to ensure that the duty of care under HASAWAis maintained.

Every company with 5 or more employees must under the Health and Safety at Work Act 1974 have a written Health and Safety policy. When counting the number of employees you must include part time employees, trainees and employees working in different salons. It is strongly recommended that every organisation should have a written policy irrespective of the number of employees.

SECTION 2 - PAGE 6

HEALTH AND SAFETY FOR HAIRDRESSERS

▲ Extract from *The Official Health & Safety Implementation Pack For Hairdressers*, available from Habia (tel. 01302 380013).

HAIRDRESSING *Training* **BOARD**

HEALTH AND SAFETY FOR HAIRDRESSERS

2. **The policy must contain the following:**

Section A : A general statement based on your obligations under the Health and Safety at Work Act and details of who is responsible for what. This statement should be signed by the most senior member of the organisation e.g. the owner or Managing Director. Remember that your employees have responsibilities under the Act to take care of the health and safety of themselves and others.

Section B : Your arrangements for health and safety are detailed in this section and these cover such areas as accident reporting, first aid and fire drills.

Section C : Your arrangements for monitoring and reviewing your policy and arrangements. This is important if health and safety is to be treated seriously.

3. **The policy, and any revisions, MUST be brought to the attention of all employees.**

An outline policy statement is attached and this can be completed and used as it is or modified to suit your particular situation.

anyone in your employment, any persons in training, casual workers and the self-employed, as well as your customers and any other visitors to your premises. The Act applies to all work activities and premises, and everyone at work has responsibilities under it.

the employer must provide:

- Safe equipment and safe systems of work
- Safe handling, storage and transportation of substances
- A safe place of work with safe access and exits
- A safe working environment with adequate welfare facilities
- The necessary training, instruction, information and supervision
- Any necessary personal protective equipment.

Under the HASAW Act, the employer has a duty of care towards the employees and all others upon the premises. All employees, under the same Act, have a duty to work in such a way so as not to endanger the health, safety or welfare of themselves or others. They must not tamper with or misuse any items provided in the interests of health and safety.

management of health and safety at work regulations 1992

The main requirement of the regulations is the necessity for the employer to carry out the assessment of risks to the health and safety of their employees and other people. Where risks are identified, it is their duty to take appropriate action to eliminate or minimise them. The employer must ensure that staff are adequately trained and fully aware of any necessary procedures. In addition to this, suitable arrangements must be made from time to time for reviewing these assessments and methods of recording the findings. The employer is required:

1. to have a written and up-to-date health and safety policy if five or more people are employed
2. to carry out risk assessment and (if more than five people are employed) record the main findings and their implications for health and safety
3. to display a valid certificate of Employer's Liability (Compulsory Insurance) Act 1969 if anyone is employed

4. to display the health and safety law poster for employees
5. to notify certain types of injuries, occupational diseases and events.

health and safety policy

All employers with five or more staff (including trainees) must have a written policy on health, safety and welfare. The policy should contain three components:

(a) a general statement indicating commitment to the Health and Safety at Work Act from the most senior person in the organisation

(b) the organisation's staffing structure which will identify each post-holder's responsibilities with regard to health and safety, and clearly show how those responsibilities will be fulfilled

(c) the arrangements and procedures that the organisation has put in place to control health and safety and to inform staff, visitors etc. about these measures, as well as the arrangements for monitoring and reviewing the policy.

risk assessment

A hazard is anything that can cause harm, such as electricity, chemicals, stock in storage etc. Risk is the chance, big or small, of harm actually being done.

As an example, consider a bottle of perm solution on a shelf. This constitutes a hazard as the liquid is alkaline, but very little risk is involved if the bottle of solution is stored properly. The risk increases when the bottle is taken down from the shelf, opened and the solution poured into another container – there is then a danger of spillage.

The Management of Health and Safety Regulations requires the employer to:

- identify the potential hazards
- assess the risk that could arise from these hazards
- identify who might be at risk
- take precautions in order to reduce or eliminate the risk
- train staff to identify and control risk
- review the above arrangements on a regular basis.

carrying out risk assessment

When undertaking a risk assessment you should take the following steps:

1. Look for the hazards

Walk around the workplace and think about what could go wrong, looking for anything that could cause harm.

Consider these typical activities and where accidents might happen:

- Stacking and storage – falling materials
- Receiving deliveries – carrying and lifting
- Dispensing chemicals – spillages and exposure to harmful substances
- Using electrical equipment – hand dryers, tongs and clippers.

2. Who might be harmed?

Decide who might be harmed by the above hazards:

- Workers
- Customers
- Other visitors to the premises.

3. How high are the risks?

Assess, for each hazard, whether there is low, medium or high risk involved.

What is the worst result that could happen? A cut finger or someone suffering permanent eye damage?

How likely is this to happen? How often is the procedure carried out? How likely is something to go wrong?

4. Are the main risks under control?

Are you taking the right precautions, and can you illuminate or reduce the risk?

COSHH Risk Assessment

Staff member responsible .... Date .... Review date

Hazards	What is the risk?	Who is at risk?	Degree of risk?	Action to reduce
Hair Colourant Permanent: Majirel, Majirouge Majimode, Majiblond	Irritant, can cause an allergenic reaction.	Staff mixing and using the product. The client if product is applied to the scalp.	Low	Use water to dilute and mop up any spillages. After mixing, the product must be used immediately and disposed of appropriately. Sensitivity test advisable.

control of substances hazardous to health regulations (COSHH) 1988

These regulations state the essential requirements for controlling exposure to hazardous substances and for protecting people who may be affected by them. The exposure to these substances may be by:

- inhalation
- ingestion
- contact with skin
- absorption through the skin
- injection into the body
- introduction into the body via open wounds.

Under the COSHH regulations, employers must carry out a risk assessment of the materials which are used within the salon. An example of the information that must be recorded is shown on page 119.

The law requires employers to:

- identify any substances within the workplace that are potentially hazardous
- assess the risk to health from exposure and record the findings
- identify who is at risk
- assess the level of risk
- provide details of the precautions or actions to take to illuminate or reduce the risk.

Guidance for good housekeeping provided by HSE:

1. simple precautions can cut exposure
2. do not store chemicals in open containers – make sure labels are not damaged, removed or covered up
3. keep dangerous chemicals locked away
4. clear up spillages quickly and safely
5. have smooth work surfaces to allow for easy cleaning
6. clean regularly
7. keep waste products in covered containers.

personal protective equipment (PPE)

Personal protective clothing and equipment should only be used as a last resort if you cannot control the exposure in other ways. See page 122 for more information on this subject.

employers' liability (compulsory insurance) act 1969

The Employers' Liability (Compulsory Insurance) Act 1969 places a duty on employers to take out and maintain approved insurance policies against liability for bodily injury or disease sustained by their employees in the course of their employment. Insurers must issue a Certificate of Insurance and employers are required to display the certificate, or a copy, at each place of business.

level of cover

An employer should insure for a minimum of £2,000,000 in respect of claims arising out of one occurrence.

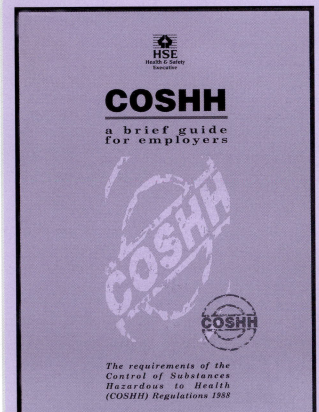

Health and Safety Executive

public liability insurance

Although not a legal requirement, it would place the business and employer in serious jeopardy without this type of cover. Modern comprehensive insurance policies developed for the sector contain an in-built cover relative to the number of personnel involved in the provision of service and treatments to clients.

the reporting of accidents (RIDDOR)

There are statutory requirements to report accidents and occupationally related diseases, and these are detailed in Reporting of Injuries, Diseases and Dangerous Occurrences Regulations 1995 (RIDDOR).

Under these regulations, the employer must notify the local enforcement officer in writing in the event of an employee who is injured at work which results in:

(a) death,

(b) a major injury,

(c) more than 24 hours in hospital, or

(d) an incapacity to work for more than three days.

Formal documentation form **F2508** for the disclosure of these occurrences under (a), (b) and (c) can be obtained from HSE Publications, PO Box 1999, Sudbury, Suffolk CO10 6FS (see Appendix 1).

recording accidents

All accidents must be recorded in the salon accident book. The recording system should be up-to-date and available for inspection.

When you are recording accident details, you will need to provide the following information:

- the full name and address of the casualty
- the occupation of the casualty
- the date of entry in the accident book
- the date and time of the accident
- accident details: location, circumstances, the work process involved
- injury details
- signature of the person making the entry.

electricity at work regulations 1989

The three main hazards resulting from electricity are contact with live parts, fire and explosion. Each year more than a thousand accidents occur at work, resulting in shock or burns, and some are even fatal. Fires started by poor installations cause many other deaths and injuries. Explosions are caused by electrical equipment igniting flammable vapours.

An employer must assess the risk from the use of electricity within the workplace. The main risk will be from faulty hand-held equipment. Therefore:

- have your electrical installation and equipment tested on a regular 12-monthly basis
- make provisions for the regular visual inspection of electrical equipment and cabling
- identify faulty/damaged equipment and remove it from access until repairs can be carried out
- make a list of all items used within the salon for easy monitoring and reviewing of maintenance.

health and safety (first aid) regulations 1981

The regulations require the employer to have appropriate equipment and facilities for administering first aid within the workplace.

You must have:

- someone who can take charge in an emergency – an appointed person must be available whenever people are at work
- a first aid box.

The appointed person will normally take charge in the event of an emergency, such as accident or fire.

They would be responsible for contacting the emergency services and possible evacuation of the premises.

The contents of the first aid box will depend on the number of staff employed and the illustration on page 122 may be used as a guide.

First Aid Box			
Employees	1–5	6–10	11–50
Contents:			
First Aid Guidance Notes	1	1	1
Individually wrapped adhesive dressings	20	20	40
Sterile eye pads	1	2	4
Sterile triangular bandages	1	2	4
Safety pins	6	6	12
Medium unmedicated dressings	3	6	8
Large unmedicated dressings	1	2	4
Extra Large unmedicated dressings	1	2	4

fire precautions

Your local fire authority will expect that:

- there are sufficient exits for everyone to get out easily
- there are clearly marked and unobstructed fire doors and escape routes
- fire doors can be easily opened from the inside whenever anyone is on the premises
- fire doors are not wedged open, they are there to stop smoke and fire spreading
- if you have a fire alarm, that it is checked regularly
- enough fire extinguishers of the right types are provided
- everyone should know what to do in the event of fire, and there is a clearly displayed fire drill
- an appointed person will raise the alarm and call the fire service.

fire precautions act 1971

Under this Act, a fire certificate is required for premises where:

(a) more than 20 people are employed on one floor at any one time, or

(b) more than 10 people are employed on different floors at any one time.

If the premises are shared with other employers, you have to include all the other people within the premises.

personal protective equipment (PPE) at work regulations 1992

The PPE Regulations 1992 require managers to make an assessment of the processes and activities carried out at work and to identify where and when special items of clothing should be worn. In most cases, the requirements of this Act will be fulfilled when compliance is made under COSHH.

In hairdressing environments, the potential hazards and dangers revolve around the task of providing hairdressing services – that is, in general, the application of hairdressing treatments and associated products.

workplace (health, safety and welfare) regulations 1992

These provide the employer with an approved code of practice for maintaining a safe, secure working environment. These regulations originally applied in full to new or modified premises and to existing premises from 1st January 1996. Up to that time, the Factories Act 1961 and the Offices, Shops and Railway Premises Act 1963 applied. The regulations cover the legal requirements in respect of the following aspects of the working environment:

- maintenance of workplace and equipment
- ventilation
- indoor temperatures
- lighting
- cleanliness and the handling of waste materials
- room dimensions
- workstations and seating
- conditions of floor and traffic routes
- falls or falling objects
- windows, doors, gates and walls
- ability to clean windows

- organisation of traffic routes, escalators and moving walkways
- sanitary conveniences, washing facilities
- drinking water
- accommodation for clothing, facilities for changing clothing
- facilities for staff to rest and to eat meals.

One of the newer amendments to this Act relates to the prevention of discomfort caused by smoking.

manual handling operations regulations 1992

These regulations apply to all occupations where manual lifting occurs. They require the employer to carry out a risk assessment of the work processes and activities that involve manual lifting. The risk assessment should address detailed aspects of the following:

- any risk of injury
- the manual movement that is involved in the task
- the physical constraints the loads incur
- the (work) environmental constraints that are incurred
- each worker's individual capabilities
- steps/remedial action to take in order to minimise risk.

provision and use of work equipment regulations (PUWER) 1992

These regulations lay down important health and safety controls on the provision and use of work equipment. They state the duties for employers, the persons in control (the users) and the self-employed. In general, they affect both new and old equipment alike. In addition to this, they cover the selection of suitable equipment, maintenance, manufacturer information, instruction and training. Specific regulations address the dangers that could arise from operation of the equipment and the potential risk of injury.

health and safety (information for employees) regulations 1989

These require all information relating to health and safety and welfare to be provided to all employees by means of posters and leaflets in the form which is approved by the Health and Safety Executive.

6

promoting the business further

part 6

promoting the
business further

public relations (courtesy of *Hairdressers Journal* magazine)

Public relations (PR) is an effective tool with which to promote your business or product. It targets the media best suited to your company image or product profile, bringing your product to the eye of the consumer and thus increasing your business potential. You can opt to handle your own PR or to employ the services of a PR consultancy.

DIY PR

Provided you have the right contacts and, more importantly, the time, it is possible to promote your business yourself. However, you should be aware that dealing with the press is not necessarily a simple case of a phone call and then a letter. It's a question of knowing whom to contact and how to get your message across. It is also a question of degree: how much promotion do you want? Is it for one specific project, or is it ongoing? If it's the latter, then be prepared for PR to take up a lot of your time.

the press

Trade and consumer press are two completely different animals. It's essential, therefore, that they are each approached in the appropriate manner.

trade press

Aimed at other businesses within the same industry, trade press is interested in news items within the trade (such as new salons, trends, techniques, etc., plus charity events and product launches). It is also a vehicle for launching new photographic collections, showcasing salon interiors and conducting business profiles.

On the whole, trade journalists tend to be the easier to deal with and more accessible – after all, they are already sympathetic to your business/product, and require your help to fill their pages!

consumer press

Aimed at the general public, consumer magazines reach a great number of people who may never have heard of you or your product, but are about to do so

through effective PR! Public relations is about editorial endorsement. This is quite different from advertising – it means the journalist is giving you magazine space without expecting any payment for it.

Such editorial endorsement can be hard to secure, but the benefits can be huge. The consumer press are not interested in new staff appointments, but they do want to know about innovative techniques, upcoming seasonal trends, latest product advancements and new salons. Happily, more and more consumer magazines are coming round to the idea that consumers are interested in their hair, and, through increased hairdressing standards and higher stylist profiles, these magazines are becoming increasingly confident in our industry.

Magazines now often have hair supplements banded to their issues, and these have to be filled.

Hair salons and product companies with effective PR are the ones who are helping to fill these supplements with hair features, by supplying press releases to the appropriate journalists which outline new techniques and products, photographic materials, seasonal trends and quotes.

employing a PR consultant

Communication on an ongoing basis with the relevant journalist is the secret to grabbing column inches. Employing a professional PR consultant can do this, and has many advantages with just one disadvantage: involving your company in an additional monthly salary! However, this 'disadvantage' can build your business, lift its profile, bring new clients through the salon door, sell more products and make you more money. So is the additional monthly salary worth it?

Certainly it is – so long as you employ the right PR consultant for your business. Ask journalists whom they would recommend. Start with the trade press or, if it's consumer coverage you're after, speak to one or two beauty editors on the magazines you think your business would be right for; journalists will feel flattered that you have asked for their opinion. Remember, journalists are dealing with professional

PR consultants on a regular basis, and will know which ones are on the ball.

When you interview a PR consultant, ask him or her to provide you with press cuttings of editorial secured with other clients. This will give you an idea of the type of editorial they are able to achieve for you – provided you have the material for them to work with!

Ask the consultant to provide a proposal for you which outlines what can be achieved for your company, and a rough time-scale. Also, ascertain approximately how much time will be spent per month on your account.

Know which other clients the consultant is working for to ensure there is no conflict of interest. While it is not necessarily a disadvantage for a PR consultant to handle clients in the same area of business (i.e. other hair salons), it certainly could be if those clients included some of your direct rivals!

Ensure you know exactly what the fee includes, so there are no hidden surprises. For example, most PR fees are quoted exclusive of expenses; however, you should know exactly what these expenses will consist of, and approximately how much they will be each month.

Ask the PR consultant how often reports are provided. A good consultant will draw up a report every four to six weeks – unless mutually agreed otherwise.

Give the PR consultant a clear brief in terms of what you expect out of the relationship – preferably in writing. This ensures a complete understanding on both sides.

A contract should be agreed on and signed by both parties. This provides for one month's notice to be given on either side. Remember, while the impossible can be achieved, miracles take a little longer! In other words, ensure you have enough material for a PR consultant to work with: inspired ideas, photographic work, etc. Be prepared to give some of your time to the consultant on a regular basis. Communication is the operative word.

Is the PR consultant on the same wavelength as you? Does he or she seem to speak your language?

No matter how good the consultant is, if there are personality clashes, then the relationship will be a difficult one.

how much will PR cost?

Fees vary and are governed by a number of factors: how much time will be spent on your business, what level of press you require (for example trade press, consumer press, local press or overseas press), how active the PR consultant will be on other aspects of the business (such as staff recruitment, advertising and staff training) and the size of your business.

A fee of £500 a month will buy basic PR consumer and trade press for a hair salon. A fee of £1,200 per month is a starting point for a product company, depending on its size. But remember that, besides time, what you are also buying is the PR consultant's invaluable knowledge of the industry and their magazine contacts. Just as your clients are buying your expertise, so you are purchasing that of another experienced and trained professional.

Public relations can be the making of your business, and so long as your mind is open to it, you secure the services of the right PR consultant, and work together with that consultant to help achieve your goals.

■ photography and photo sessions

Why do it? (courtesy of *Hairdressers Journal* magazine)

The power of a good photograph is undeniable. It instantly says more about your work and the image you want to project than any free editorial or paid-for advertising will. However, while fun, photo sessions are not easy. They can be time-consuming, expensive and, sometimes, disappointing if not properly coordinated.

So how do you go about things? First, ask yourself why you want to invest in an expensive photo session. Is it to attract more clients into the salon through coverage in the consumer press? Is it to raise your

Mahogany

industry profile via the trade press? Or is it for salon advertising?

Next, study the magazines and newspapers in which you hope to have your work published and check the sort of photographs they use. Individual titles will have a distinctive 'house style': the type of work published in *Cosmopolitan* and *Elle* is very different from that in *Vogue* and *Tatler* or teenage magazines, and a world apart from that in local newspapers.

putting it together

Once you've decided on the look you're going to go for, start to create your photographic team.

the model

Picking a suitable model can be a tricky task. A common mistake is to choose a pretty girl with unsuitable hair or vice versa; ideally she should have a combination of both. And remember, a conventionally pretty face isn't always photogenic, so study each model's photographic portfolio carefully:

■ Look for regular features and bright, clear eyes. Avoid prominent chins and noses, over-full lips or dark circles under the eyes. The skin should be clear (even the most skilful of make-up artists won't be able to disguise completely obvious blemishes), and she should have a long, slim, unlined neck and a good profile to give the photographer maximum scope.

■ Ensure the hair suits the type of work you plan to do. Most professional models won't allow you to cut, colour or perm their hair, so your choice needs to be the right length, shade, texture and style. The model must also have the right features to fit your look – a sweet face is no good if you want an aggressive punk image.

■ Always use professional models.

■ Call a casting, take Polaroids of all the girls you like and make notes to refresh your memory later.

■ Don't book more than four models for a one day session – rushed results won't work.

■ **Never** cut, colour or perm a professional model's hair (even if she agrees) without checking with her agency first.

the photographer

Always opt for someone who specialises in hair, beauty or fashion photography. See as many as you can, with portfolios, to check their ideas are in tune with yours. Confirm the booking in writing and brief him or her in detail on the image and 'feeling' you are aiming for.

the make-up artist

A good make-up artist is vital – bad make-up will ruin a shot. If you can afford it, always use a professional, but don't ask for the impossible – a make-up artist, however good, can't completely change a model's face. Research and brief a make-up artist as you would a photographer.

clothes and accessories

Decide on the time of year you hope to have the photographs published, and bear in mind that most monthly magazines work three months ahead. What type of clothes work best? Obviously this depends on the image you want to achieve and whether you are working with a professional stylist. If you don't want your shots to date too quickly then go for neutral fashions that don't scream out a particular season.

Mahogany

Be decisive and don't settle for second best. If you're not completely happy with a shot, say so nicely. And always check through the camera: you'll be surprised how different something looks through the lens.

Keep backgrounds simple so as not to distract from the hair. The golden rule is slightly darker for blondes, and lighter for darker hair so the shape shows up more clearly. Make sure hair is well-lit and the photographer isn't indulging in some fancy lighting effects that show off his or her artistry rather than yours.

Necklines should be simple and jewellery effective. But don't overload – if in doubt, leave out.

plan of action

Think about the designs and put together a 'story board' by cutting out images you like from magazines. Once you've decided on the styles, work out how you are going to achieve them. By creating a theme for your collection, you'll have more chance of greater coverage.

Teamwork is the key to a successful photographic session, so let those involved know exactly what they'll be doing. Remember, studio time is valuable; do any major hair preparation work before the shoot.

Draw up a list of the equipment and products you'll need, and check them off when packing your session tool kit. The general rule is to take everything – and then add anything else that might come in handy!

on the day

Have a clear idea of the looks you want to create but have in mind several alternatives as back-up. Pay attention to detail and make sure you see a Polaroid of every style before the photographer starts snapping in earnest. Picking up on faults not obvious to the naked eye isn't always easy; those to look out for include gaps in the style, stray hairs on clothes/face, rumpled clothes, pins showing or too much product/make-up.

what's the price?

Cost is a four-letter word – so take a deep breath here. If using a top professional photographer and shooting in London, the minimum for PR rates will be £1,000 (and the price rises according to the photographer's fame). Then you've got the cost of the studio, models, make-up artist and travel expenses on top. As with most things, it's cheaper outside London.

Keep a tight control on budget as costs can easily escalate. Often, photographers' quotes only cover their time on the day, so check if heating, lighting and food are on top. Check also film, developing and reprint costs, and remember to be clear about how you intend to use your shots. Prices can change depending on whether you use the photographs for one-off editorial, general PR or advertising.

Get the agreed charges in writing beforehand, and don't try to pull a fast one. If you say the shots are for one-off editorial, but use them for PR instead and get found out, you could be sued. And that's expensive.

the size is right

Size matters. Individual publications will specify how they prefer to receive photographic material, but those most widely accepted are:

■ *Prints*: shot on black-and-white or colour film, the best size is 10 in × 8 in (though 7 in × 5 in is acceptable)

Patrick Cameron

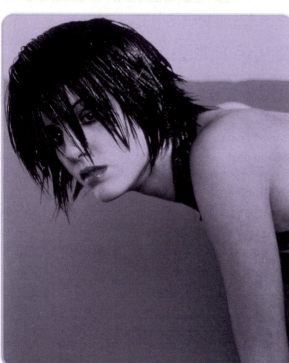

Mahogany

■ *Colour transparencies*: medium-format 2.25 in square, or large-format 5 in × 4 in transparencies, particularly if you're hoping for a cover (these films are more expensive). Regular 35 mm is also well accepted but these images can sometimes become grainy if blown up fairly big.

Magazines always prefer original transparencies as they reproduce better. However, these can get lost or misplaced, so it's best to get good duplicates to send out; hang on to your originals. The exception here is if your photograph is to be used on a cover.

Never send glass-mounted slides. Journalists hate them as the glass always breaks (no matter how carefully packed) and scratches the transparencies, so making the image unpublishable.

■ hairdressing competitions

Entering hairdressing competitions can be great fun and a great motivator for your staff. It is, however, very challenging and requires a lot of personal discipline, dedication and thorough practice in order to achieve the right look that will catch the eye of the adjudicators.

Competitions vary enormously – from local and regional to national – and will also vary in the way that entrants take part.

For example, the L'Oreal Colour trophy, a national competition, is initially short-listed at a regional level by photographic entry. Only when a styling team is selected and invited to take part at the regional finals will entrants have to demonstrate their work 'live' against the clock. Conversely, National Hairdressing Federation competitions at regional levels allow all comers to participate on the competition floor. Finalists from individual regions are then invited to take part at national level. The British Hairdressing Awards (owned and presented by the *Hairdressers Journal* and sponsored by Schwarzkopf) are again a national competition that is short-listed by photographic entry (see below for more details of these Awards). In this competition, entrants participate in a variety of categories ranging from Regional, Avant-garde, Artistic Team and London to British Hairdresser.

Many hairdressing organisations, colleges and major manufacturers run or sponsor competitions. If it's something that you would wish your salon to be involved with, encourage your salon to run an in-house competition first. This is a good way of 'acclimatising' your staff to the pressures of competing.

The Hairdressing Training Board has issued the following tips to help you get started before you step on to the competition floor:

- Watch the trade press for news about when and where competitions are taking place.
- Go along to competitions and watch what happens. See what type of work is successful in competitions and keep an eye on emerging trends and fashions.
- Ask trainers and tutors for advice. Also take advice from people who have entered or know about competitions.
- Read the rules carefully and know exactly what is required.
- Take time to find exactly the right model, one with the right type of hair, the right age and with looks that fit into the competition rules. A beautiful girl with good deportment helps considerably, but if her hairline is not up to scratch she may put you out of the competition.
- Understand that competition work is very different from salon work. Colouring, in particular, can often be a lot stronger in a competition environment than that which would be used in the salon.

Regular competitors stress the importance of preparation:

- Check and prepare your equipment
- Take time to find the right model, particularly if you are trying to express a specific image or theme
- Product knowledge and application are imperative, never attempt to style a model's hair without testing the products' effects on her hair beforehand
- Practise, practise and practise.

Regular entry to competition keeps you up-to-date; you get a feel for the emerging undercurrents, fashions and trends which is vitally important. The motivation gained by attending competitions is infectious if it is then passed on to younger members of staff. Competitions give you the opportunity to see what your competitors are doing. There is always something to be learnt by watching other salon teams and stylists at work.

'live' competition (on the day)

You have prepared your model and you have practised the look for hours. Now the day of the competition has arrived. Stage fright has struck; keep calm, there is nothing to worry about, everyone including the 'great names' suffer from nerves at this time. And not just the stylists but the models too!

The style you do must conform to the competition rules. For example, if a day style is required, don't go over the top with elaborate 'hair up' or hair ornaments. If it's free style, a wider choice is allowed.

Once you and your fellow competitors have finished your models, you'll be asked to leave the floor so the judges can take over. These people, who are normally qualified hairdressers, hair and beauty journalists and, occasionally, previous winners, choose the most competently designed and dressed head of hair. Depending on the type of competition, the judges will award points covering all aspects of style ranging from technical detail, shape and movement to use of colour and artistic adaptation.

■ the British Hairdressing Awards

The British Hairdressing Awards were created in 1985 and, during their lifetime, they have grown into hairdressing's most prestigious and high-profile competition. Almost every top salon in the nation enters the Awards; for the winners, it can be the highlight of – or indeed the launch pad for – a long and glittering career. In fact, the Awards have been the making of many of our top stylists, not to mention the raising of standard of hairdressing photographic work overall in this country.

Since 1990, the British Hairdressing Awards have been owned and presented by *Hairdressers Journal* (previously, the event belonged to its sister publication, *Hair And Beauty* magazine). Schwarzkopf UK, however, have been the exclusive sponsor since the Awards' inception.

how do they work?

There are 16 categories of Awards: eight regional categories; six specialist categories (Newcomer and Artistic Team of the Year, plus Men's, Afro, Avant-garde and Session Hairdresser of the Year); the more recent British Film Hairdresser of the Year; and the ultimate Award, British Hairdresser of the Year.

Entrants are judged primarily on photographic work – they are required to supply four prints for an initial judging session, then another four if they make it through to the finals – and on a résumé of the past year's show and seminar work they have conducted, plus trade and consumer press coverage they have obtained.

You can enter any category you like (so long as you meet the relevant requirements), except the British Film, Session and British categories. The winner of British Film is determined by experts within that particular field; finalists in Session and British are nominated by a panel of trade and consumer hair and beauty experts. Session stylists are judged on their professional portfolio; British finalists are judged on their portfolio of eight photographic prints and, separately, on a résumé of their contribution to raising the profile of the British hairdressing industry over the past 12 months. On occasions, it has been the latter that has decided the overall winner.

There are two judging stages. First-round entries are judged by members of the British Hairdressing Awards Hall of Fame – hairdressers who have won an Award three times, plus honorary members, including Vidal Sassoon and Robert Lobetta. They have the invariably difficult task of whittling down each category to six finalists, examining each portfolio for technical expertise and commercial flair.

The second-round judging takes place when finalists have submitted their additional four prints, and when nominees in the Session and British categories have submitted their portfolios and résumés. At this stage, the jury consists of around 30 prominent hair and beauty experts – editors of consumer and trade magazines, for example, dignitaries from hairdressing associations, and leading salon owners who have not participated in the Awards themselves. Theirs are the scores that determine the overall winner in each category.

And, finally, bringing months of nail-biting tension to an end, the results are announced at the British Hairdressing Awards presentation ceremony at the end of November in a top West End hotel. This is the time when the hairdressing industry turns out in its most sumptuous and glittering force – national press and TV cameras now cover the event as a matter of course. For some of the finalists, the evening will inevitably end in disappointment. For 16 others, however, it will mark the beginning of a year of celebration and widespread recognition.

how can I win?

Ultimately, there is no recipe for guaranteed Awards' success – who can predict what will catch the eye of the judges? However, experience shows that following certain photographic guidelines could possibly increase your chances of winning.

be professional with your portfolio

Using a professional photographer, make-up artist and, above all, professional models is a must. Gone are the days when you could get away with taking four snapshots of your best friend with your back garden as a location. (Admittedly, some salons still do this, but they never make the finals.) The more successful Awards' entrants have long since wised up to the fact that an initial investment in people who will reflect their own hairdressing work to best effect usually reaps dividends later on down the line.

'It would never occur to me not to use a professional model,' says Trevor Sorbie, 'even though they can cost me an arm and a leg.' And has the principle paid off? Well, Trevor has won British Hairdresser of the Year no less than four times so far.

work to a theme

There is a theory (and recent results would seem to bear it out) that a portfolio of pictures shot specifically for the Awards stands a better chance of success than a random collection of prints culled from various shoots throughout the year. Certainly, judges seem to respond better to a set of pictures where there is an overall theme – all hair up, for example, or all black-and-white shots as they tend to be easier on the eye and 'work' as a collection. Also, it shows you've really thought about your entry, and how best to show off your talent.

don't go overboard

With the exception of the Avant-garde category, it's a pretty safe bet that the judges will be looking for technical excellence – but also commercial relevance. In other words, fantasy hairstyles will not win you marks. Instead, try to have your pictures reflect current hair trends, or at least display images that your clients could actually respond to. That means wearable styles, great colour, beautiful perms and good all-round suitability to the tastes and fashions of the New Millennium.

■ the British Hairdressing Business Awards

The British Hairdressing Business Awards (BHBA) is another competition that is run by the *Hairdresser's Journal International*. Although a recent newcomer to the industry this competition sponsored by various manufacturers focuses specifically upon business as opposed to hairdressing excellence.

The BHBA was launched to recognise business flair, commercial performance and customer service. Successful finalists can earn the respect of their peers and clients, as well as motivating the salon team. The final of the awards takes place each year in September, although the entry submissions are required by the beginning of June. Prospective entrants have a range of categories to choose from. The categories are:

- Customer Care Award (sponsored by Wella)
- Manager of the Year (sponsored by L'Oréal)
- Salon team of the Year (sponsored by Clynol)
- Innovation of the Year (sponsored by Schwarzkopf)
- The Training Award (sponsored by Wella)
- Independent Salon – Business Newcomer (sponsored by HJ)
- Junior of the year (sponsored by L'Oréal)
- Salon of the Year – Multiple (sponsored by Schwarzkopf)
- Marketing Initiative Award (sponsored by Wella)
- Salon Design Award (sponsored by Welonda)
- Salon of the Year – Independent (sponsored by Clynol)
- Retailer of the Year (sponsored by Tresemmé)
- Business Director of the Year (sponsored by HJ)

how to enter

Entrants are required to submit a written presentation based upon their chosen award. The entry is expected to be clearly presented, well structured, visually pleasing and easy for the judging panel to read.

the judging

The judging takes place over two days, which is then followed up by a 'mystery visit' and phone calls to the finalists. There are two judging panels, one is made up from representatives of each of the sponsoring companies and the other panel is from the 'business world', these judges have backgrounds in marketing, design and training. Each application is marked by a separate judge, the totals are accumulated and the successful short-list is drawn up. The judges will be looking for:

- clear and concise information
- proof of any claims made
- innovative ideas that have proved to be successful
- well thought out imaginative presentation.

The culmination takes place at a 'top' London hotel. The excitement reaches fever pitch, as the short-listed finalists enjoy an evening of entertainment, good food and then, finally, the presentations are made. Winners of the business awards can expect a lot of P.R. interest and general business promotion, as they reap the rewards of demonstrating their particular 'head' for business.

appendix 1: legislation and useful addresses

■ legislation

UK statutes and regulations

Asylum and Immigration Act 1996
Employment Rights Act 1996
Employment Rights (Dispute Resolution) Act 1998
Equal Pay Act 1970
Disability Discrimination Act 1995
Health and Safety at Work etc. Act 1974
Race Relations Act 1976
Sex Discrimination Acts 1975 (as amended)
Trade Union Labour Relations Act 1992
Transfer of Undertakings (Protection of Employment)
    Regulations 1981

European directives

Acquired Rights Directive
Equal Treatment Directive
Working Time Directive

useful addresses and telephone numbers

This section contains details of organisations giving general advice. You may also be able to contact specialist helplines for your professional area.

ACAS
Brandon House
180 Borough High Street
London SE1 1LW
    Website: **www.acas.org.uk**
Look in the phone book for details of your local office

Amalgamated Engineering and Electrical Union (AEEU)
Hayes Court
West Common Road
Bromley
Kent BR2 7AU
    Tel: 0208-462 7755
    Fax. 0208-315 8234
    Email: **j.staples@headoffice.aecu.org.uk**
    Website: **www.aecu.org.uk**

Benefits Enquiry Line
    Tel: 0800-882200

British Association for Counselling (BAC)
1 Regent Place
Rugby
Warks CV21 2PJ
    Tel: 01788-578328 (Information line)
    Fax: 01788-562189
    Email: **bac@bac.co.uk**

Citizens Advice Bureau
Look in the phone book for details of your local office

Commission for Racial Equality (CRE)
Elliott House
10–12 Allington Street
London SW1E 5EH
    Tel: 0207-828 7022
    Fax: 0207-630 7605
    Website: **www.open.gov.uklcrel crehome.htm**

Confederation of British Industry (CBI)
Centre Point
103 Oxford Street
London WC1A 1DU
  Tel: 0207-379 7400
  Fax: 0207-240 0988
  Website: **www.cbi.org.uk**

Contributions Agency
Look in the phone book for details of your local office

Contributions Agency International Services
Longbenton
Newcastle-upon-Tyne NE98 1YX
  Tel: 0191-225 481 1 (Helpdesk)
  Fax: 0191-225 7800
  Email: **www.inlandrevenue.gov.uk**

Department of Trade and Industry
Advance Notification Section
Redundancy Payments Offices
Hagley House
83–85 Hagley Road
Birmingham B16 8QG
  Tel: 0121-456 4411
  Fax: 0121-454 7881

For giving advance notice of redundancies:

Disability Alliance (DAERA)
Universal House
88–94 Wentworth Street
London E1 7SA
  Tel: 0207-247 8776
  0207-247 8763 (Rights advice line)
  Mons, Weds 2–4 pm
  Fax: 0207-247 8765

DTI Employment Relations Directorate
1 Victoria Street
London SW1H 0ET
  Tel: 0207-215 5985
  Fax: 0207-215 2635
  Website: **www.dti.gov.uk**

DTI Publications Orderline
1 Victoria Street
London SW1H 0ET
  Tel: 0870-1502500
  Fax: 0870-1502333
  Email: **dtipubs@echristian.co.uk**
  Website: **www.dti.gov.uk**

Employment Agency Standards Office
Department of Trade and Industry
1 Victoria Street
London SW1H OET
  Tel: 0645-555105 (Helpline)
  Fax: 0207-215 2636

Employment Appeal Tribunal
Central Office
58 Victoria Embankment
London EC4Y 0DS
  Tel: 0207-273 1041
  Fax: 0207-273 1045

Equal Opportunities Commission (EOC)
Overseas House
Quay Street
Manchester M3 3HN
  Tel: 0161-833 9244
  Fax: 0161-835 1657
  Website: **www.eoc.org.uk**

Eye Care Information Service
PO Box 3597
London SE1 6DY
  Send an SAE marked 'VDU information' for leaflets

Fair Employment Commission (FEC)
Andras House
60 Great Victoria Street
Belfast BT2 7BB
  Tel: 02890-500600
  Fax: 02890-331544

FCO Migration and Visa Division
  Tel: 0207-238 463314664
  0207-238 4639 (Leaflet orderline)

FCO Travel Advice Unit
  Tel: 0207-238 450314504

Foreign and Commonwealth Office (FCO)
1 Palace Street
London SW1E 5HE
  Website: **www.fco.gov.uk**

GMB Union
Head Office
22–24 Worple Road
Wimbledon
London SW19 4DD
  Tel: 0208-947 3131
  Fax: 0208-944 6552
  Website: **www.gmb.org.uk**

Health and Safety Executive (HSE)
Information Centre
Broad Lane
Sheffield S3 7HQ
  Tel: 0541-545500 (Information line)
Look in the phone book for details of your local office

Home Office
  Tel: 0208-649 7878 (Employers' helpline)

HSE Publications
PO Box 1999
Sudbury
Suffolk CO10 6FS
  Tel: 01787-881165 (Publications order line)

Immigration and Nationality Directorate
Lunar House
Wellesley Road
Croydon
Surrey CR9 2BY
  Tel: 0208-686 0688 (Immigration and residency
  enquiries)
  Fax: 0208-760 1181
  Website: **www.homeoffice.gov.uk/ind/hpg.htni**

Industrial Society
Peter Runge House
3 Carlton House Terrace
London SW1 SDG
  Tel: 0207-479 1000
  Fax: 0207-479 1111
  Email: **infoserve@indusoc.demon.co.uk**
  Website: **www.indsoc.co.uk**

Industrial Tribunal
  Tel: 0345-959775 (Enquiry line)
Mon to Fri 9 am–5 pm

Inland Revenue
  Website: **www.inlandrevenue.gov.uk**
Look in the phone book for details of your local office

JobCentre
Look in the phone book for details of your local office

appendix 2: business, inland revenue and H.M. customs and excise information

■ helplines

New Employers Helpline (Inland Revenue)
This helpline is specifically for new employers, who are taking on employees for the first time, to obtain general help and advice on employment, or for employers who have been employing staff within the last three years to obtain assistance:

New Employers Helpline 0845 6143143

Employers Helpline (Inland Revenue)
Ideal for employers who have general enquiries regarding Tax, National Insurance or basic VAT registration. This covers employers' PAYE, P11D expenses and benefits, statutory maternity pay and statutory sickness pay:

Employers Helpline 0345 143143

Business Link
A national network of information and advice centres which provides a single access point for local businesses. All the key support agencies, the training and enterprise council, the local enterprise agency, the chamber of commerce and local authorities, may be contacted locally. Alternatively call

0345 567765 for details of your nearest Business Link.

H.M. Customs and Excise
For information on VAT or publications or videos relating to VAT procedures, call your local VAT office (consult your phone book for details of your local office).

■ where can I get leaflets and forms for tax and other information?

Your local Tax Office or Inland Revenue Enquiry Centre will supply you with leaflets and forms about tax and some National Insurance leaflets. Their addresses are in your local phone book under 'Inland Revenue'. Most offices are open to the public from 8.30 am to 4.30 pm from Monday to Friday. Some are also open outside these hours.

Some leaflets you may find useful are:

IR List	*Catalogue of leaflets and booklets*
IR56/N139	*Employed or self-employed?*
IR120	*You and the Inland Revenue*
IR 125	*Using your own car for work*
IR160	*Inland Revenue enquiries under Self Assessment*
CWG1	*Employer's quick guide to PAYE and NICs*
CWG2	*Employer's further guide to PAYE and NICs*
CWL2	*National Insurance contributions for self-employed people. Class 2 and Class 44*

In addition, the Inland Revenue have produced the following leaflets on Self Assessment:

SA/BK3	*Self Assessment. A guide to keeping records for the self-employed*
SA/BK4	*Self Assessment. A general guide to keeping records*
SA/BK5	*Self Assessment. Electronic version of the tax return*

SA/BK6 *Self Assessment. Penalties for late tax returns*

SA/BK7 *Self Assessment. Surcharges for late payment of tax*

SA/BK8 *Self Assessment. Your guide*

Your nearest Inland Revenue (NI Contributions) Office will supply you with leaflets and forms relating to National Insurance Contributions. Some leaflets you may find useful are:

CA01 *National Insurance contributions for employees*

CA02 *National Insurance contributions for self-employed people with small earnings*

CA04 *National Insurance contributions. Class 2 and Class 3 Direct Debit. The easier way to pay*

CA07 *National Insurance contributions – unpaid and late paid contributions*

CA08 *National Insurance contributions. Voluntary contributions*

CA09 *National Insurance contributions for widows*

CA11 *National Insurance contributions for share fishermen*

CA13 *National Insurance contributions for married women*

CA25 *National Insurance contributions for agencies and agency-supplied workers*

CA72 *National Insurance contributions. Deferring payment*

CWG1 *Employer's quick guide to PAYE and NICs*

CWG2 *Employer's further guide to PAYE and NICs*

CWL2 *National Insurance contributions for self-employed people. Class 2 and Class 4*

FB30 *Self-employed? A guide to National Insurance contributions and Social Security benefits*

N138 *Social Security abroad* (NIL38 in Northern Ireland)

N1132 *National Insurance abroad. A guide for employers of people working abroad*

PP3 *Personal pensions for the self-employed*

Your local VAT Business Advice Centre will supply you with public notices and forms about VAT. They are listed under 'Customs and Excise' in the phone book. Most offices are open to the public from 9.30 am to 4 pm, Monday to Friday. Some notices you may find useful are:

700 *The VAT Guide*

700/12 *Filling in your VAT return*

700115 *The Ins and Outs of VAT*

700121 *Keeping records and accounts*

700141 *Late registration penalty*

731 *Cash accounting*

732 *Annual accounting*

999 *Catalogue of publications*

Full details about registration are in the following VAT Notices:

700/1 *Should I be registered for VAT? (available in clearprint)*

700/1A *Should I be registered for VAT? – Distance selling*

700/1B *Should I be registered for VAT? – Acquisitions*

For information on Excise and Inland Customs, see:

206 *Excise Traders*

501 *Guide to Exports*

502 *Guide to Imports*

appendix 3: investors in people and the nationally approved salon campaign

investors in people (IIP)

There are many quality issue campaigns, but IIP and NASC are the most applicable for salons looking to future business needs.

Investors in People is the national standard setting the level of good practice for training and development of people to achieve business goals. The Standard was developed during 1990 by the National Training Task Force in partnership with leading national business, personnel, professional and employee organisations. The work was supported by the Employment Department and was extensively tested during 1991 by Training and Enterprise Councils and Local Enterprise Companies (LECs).

The Standard provides a national framework for improving business performance and competitiveness, through a planned approach to setting and communicating business objectives and developing people to meet these objectives. The result simply combines what people can do and are motivated to do whilst matching what the organisation needs them to do.

An investor in people:

- Is committed to training and developing all employees to help achieve business goals
- Regularly reviews the training and development needs of all employees
- Takes action to train and develop individuals from when they join and throughout their employment
- Assesses investment in training and development to ensure success and seek continuous improvement.

All organisations face new challenges in an increasingly competitive environment which in turn:

- Raises customer expectations
- Increases competition
- Increases the penalty for failure

(for further information for IIP contact your local Training & Enterprise council).

nationally approved salon campaign (NASC)

This initiative, administered through the HTB (Hairdressing Training Board) sets out to identify and accredit salons with national recognition. The campaign's aim is to help raise customer perception whilst acknowledging high standards.

A Nationally Approved Salon can expect:

- improved client confidence
- to keep clients happy and stylists busy

- to attract new clients and keep them
- to have more local salon promotion
- national consumer awareness of the Approved Salon Campaign
- to differentiate itself from the competition
- to access up-to-date information on training and education.

It is also considered that recognition as a Nationally Approved Salon can help with staff recruitment and retention.

Salons looking to achieve this recognition would need to meet the following criteria:

- All staff having the minimum hairdressing qualification recognised in the UK (NVQ/SVQ Level 2 in Hairdressing or equivalent)
- Salon owner or Manager with 7 years' management experience or a recognised management qualification
- Senior hairdressers having or undertaking the advanced hairdressing qualification (NVQ/SVQ Level 3 in Hairdressing or equivalent)
- State Registration for one Senior stylist or Manager
- Public Liability and Treatment Insurance to protect clients
- Adhering to Health and Safety and Equal Opportunity legislation
- Displaying a formal procedure for clients who wish to register their praise or complaint
- A written training plan to keep staff skills up-to-date
- Clients being informed when a trainee is undertaking treatment upon them.

For more information regarding NASC contact:

The Hairdressing Training Board (HTB)

2nd Floor Fraser House

Nether Hall Road

Doncaster DN1 2PH

Tel: 01302-380000

Fax: 01302-380028

Email: nas@salon.org.uk

appendix 4: recommended reading list

Subject	Title	Author(s)	Publisher
Accounting	Frank Wood's Book-keeping and Accounts	Frank Wood and Sheila Robinson	Financial Times Prentice Hall
	Mastering Accounting Skills	Margaret Nicholson	Macmillan
Business	How to Set Up and Run Your Own Business	The Daily Telegraph Series	Kogan Page
	Small Business Handbook	Philip and Sandra Webb	Financial Times Prentice Hall
HR	Human Resource Management and Development: Current Issues and Themes	John Kempton	Macmillan
	Mastering Human Resources	Kelvin Cheatle	Macmillan
	People Management	Institute of Management (I.M.)	Hodder & Stoughton
	Personal Effectiveness and Career Development	Institute of Management (I.M.)	Hodder & Stoughton
Interviews and Appraisal	Taking Appraisals and Interviews	Jean Civil	Ward Lock
Management	Leadership and the One Minute Manager	Kenneth Blanchard	Harper Collins
	Management: How To Do It	John and Shirley Payne	Gower
	Managing for the Investors In People	Peter Taylor and Bob Thackwray	Kogan Page
	Mastering Basic Management (3rd edition)	E.C. Eyre and Richard Pettinger	Macmillan
	Mastering Customer Relations	Roger Cartwright	Macmillan
	Motivating Employees	Anne Bruce and James Pepitone	McGraw-Hill

Subject	Title	Author	Publisher
Psychology	*Body Language*	Allan Pease	Sheldon Press
Stress Management	*Stress Management Techniques*	Dr Vernon Coleman	Mercury
Tax	*Self Assessment for the Small Business and Self-Employed*	Niki Chesworth	Kogan Page
Time Management	*ABC Time Tips*	Merrill Douglas	McGraw-Hill
	More Time Less Stress	Martin Scott	Random House

index